Persian Alphabet for Beginners

الفبای فارسی

Learn Farsi to Fluency and Beyond

By:
Hamid Eslamian

Persian - English

Persian Alphabet for Beginners

Published by Persian Learning Center

Web: www.persianbell.com

Email: info@persianbell.com

Copyright © 2023 by the Persian Learning Center. All rights reserved. No part of this publication may be reproduced, stored in a retrieval system, or transmitted in any form or by any means, electronic, mechanical, photocopying, recording, scanning, or otherwise, except as permitted under Section 107 or 108 of the 1976 United States Copyright Ac, without permission of the author.

All inquiries should be addressed to the Persian Learning Center.

ISBN: 978-1-63620-900-5

Persian Learning Center

We are the Persian Learning Center and we have been teaching Farsi and writing Farsi book here in Dallas, TX since 2016. We believe a simple way to stay sharp throughout our lives is learning a second language, because we neglect to train our brains. you can learn and speak Persian language with our method quickly and easily, even if you found it impossible before. We started teaching and learning Farsi, because some of the next generation of population who immigrated, need to know the legacy of last generation. Also, we are looking forward teaching the learners that have related to Persia culture. I would like to personally invite you to call and have a free session with us.

www.persianbell.com

A Beginners' Book for Learning the Persian Alphabet & Script

If you find yourself overwhelmed trying to study and review thousands of Persian phrases and vocabulary words or are struggling to speak Persian with native speakers, try this book! This is not basic Persian for beginners, but a book that will teach you how to learn Persian the smart way and discover how you can easily conquer the Persian language using highly effective methods and strategies used by polyglots.

Learning Persian can open opportunities for travel, for work, or just to meet new people and understand their lives in a new way as well as open doors to Persian culture. Farsi is also considered a "critically needed" language by the U.S. government.

In the Persian Alphabet book, readers are taught expressions and learn the Farsi writing system. Language learners will find these lessons clear and easy to follow. In the end, you'll be able to read and write the 32-letter Persian alphabet and understand short sentences, express your basic needs.

Inside this book is a system that allows you to learn and never forget thousands of new Persian vocabulary words that you encounter from any Persian language source of your choice. Whether you are at basic Persian for beginners' level or intermediate levels, use this book to help you learn Persian to fluency faster and easier starting today!

Learn Persian Smarter and Faster Starting Today!

www.persianbell.com

CONTENTS

STARTING FROM ZERO 9

Persian Alfabet 11
Letter alef: 13
Letter be: 14
Letter dal: 16
Letter nun: 18
Letter re: 20
Letter mim: 22
Letter sin: 24
Letter te: 26
Letter vav: 28
Letter ye: 30
Letter ze: 32
Letter kaf: 34
Letter pe: 36
Letter he: 38
Letter shin: 40
Letter fe: 42
Letter khe: 44
Letter che: 46
Letter ghaf: 48
Leter gaf: 50
Letter jim: 52
Letter lam: 54
Letter zhe: 56
Leter sad: 58
Letter he: 60
Letter eyn: 62
Letter se: 64
Letter zad: 66
Letter gheyn: 68

- Letter ta: 70
- Letter za: 72
- Letter zal: 74
- Letter ham-ze: 76

LEARN LIKE A NATIVE 79

- Vowels: 80
- Multiphones letters 82
- Same pronunciation 83
- Arabic Leters: 84
- Initial hamze: 84
- Tanvin 86
- Tashdid 86
- Genitive 86
- Gender 87
- Accusative case 88
- Conjunction 89
- Interrogative 90
- Plural of Nouns 92
- Conjugation 93
- Convert letters: 94
- Vav 95
- Contraction: 95
- Year 96
- Days of the week: 97
- Colors 98
- Numbers: 99
- Learning Time 102
- Mathematical sign: 105

READING AND WRITING 107

- Text 1 108
- Text 2 109

www.persianbell.com

TEXT 3	110
TEXT 4	111
TEXT 5	112
TEXT 6	113
TEXT 7	114
TEXT 8	115
TEXT 9	116
TEXT 10	117
NEW WORDS	**119**

Starting from Zero

Persian script is composed of Arabic letters written from right to left. The alphabet consists of 32 letters, most of which are joinable from left and right, and have both a full form and a short form. Eight of them have single forms. Persian letters are normally joined to one another. Therefore, the appearance of a letter changes depending on its position: beginning (joined on the left), middle (joined on both sides), end (joined on the right) of a word and some letters are written in complete isolation.

This writing style is also implemented on computers. Whenever the Farsi script is typed, the computer connects the letters to each other.

Five letters are considered as multiphones, the remaining letters having a single sound each.

The regular letters used for written Farsi stand for some different sounds. It is usually difficult to tell how a word is pronounced just by looking at how it is spelled. Therefore, it is useful to show the pronunciation of each word separately, using a system of symbols in which each symbol stands for one sound only. The pronunciations of letters and words are given within two slashes. This book uses a simple spelling system to show how letters and words are pronounced, using the symbols listed below:

Summary of the pronunciation of the Persian letters:

Symbol	Example	Symbol	Example
a	hat/hat/	sh	she/shi/
â	cup/câp/	l	loss/lâs/
ay	time/tâym/	m	move/muv/
b	Book/bok/	n	need/nid/
c	Cell/sel/	o	home/houm/
ch	church/church/	ô	coat/côt/
d	dog/dâg/	oo	mood/mud/
e	pen/pen/	u	mood/mud/
ey	name/neym/	p	park/park/
f	free/fri/	r	rise/rais/
g	get/get/	s	seven/seven/
gh	Merci/meghsi/(French)	n	nation/neyshen/
h	his/hiz/	t	train/treyn/
i	feet/fit/	v	vary/vari/
iyu	cute/kiyut/	y	yet/yet/
j	jeans/jinz/	z	zipper/zipper/
k	key/ki/	zh	measure/mezher/
kh	loch/lakh/	'	/ta'lim/ تعلیم

www.persianbell.com

Persian Alfabet

Shape	Name		Sound		Example
ا/آ	الف	alef	-/'/â	[ʔ/Ø/æ/Dː]	bar
ب	بِ	be	b	[b]	book
پ	پِ	pe	p	[p]	pen
ت	تِ	te	t	[t]	ten
ث	ثِ	se	s	[s]	so
ج	جیم	jim	j	[dʒ]	joke
چ	چِ	che	č	[ʧ]	chin
ح	حِ	he	h	[h]	hand
خ	خِ	khe	x	[x]	loch
د	دال	dâl	d	[d]	Do
ذ	ذال	Zâl	z	[z]	Zoo
ر	رِ	re	r	[r]	Red
ز	زِ	ze	z	[z]	Zip
ژ	ژِ	zhe	ž	[ʒ]	Measure
س	سین	sin	s	[s]	So
ش	شین	shin	š	[ʃ]	Shape

ص	صاد	sâd	s	[s]	So
ض	ضاد	zâd	z	[z]	Zoo
ط	طا	tâ	t	[t]	Ten
ظ	ظا	zâ	z	[z]	Zoo
ع	عین	ain	'	[ʔ/Ø]	Uh-oh
غ	غین	ghain	q	[G/ɣ]	Merci
ف	فِ	fe	f	[f]	Fat
ق	قاف	ghâf	q	[G/ɣ]	Merci
ک	کاف	kâf	k	[k]	Cat
گ	کاف	gâf	g	[g]	Go
ل	لام	lâm	l	[l]	Leg
م	میم	mim	m	[m]	Me
ن	نون	non	n	[n]	No
و	واو	vâv	v/o/u/ow	[v/uː/o/ow]	Voice/zoom
ه	ه	he	h/e/a	[h/Ø/e/æ]	Hand/set
ی	ی	ye	y/i/â/ey	[j/i/Dː/ej]	Yes/see
ء	همزه	hamzeh	'	[ʔ/Ø]	Uh-oh

آ ا

Letter alef:

Letters /alef/ has the four sounds /ā, a, e, o/

Alef is a vowel. With the sign ~, called /mad/ it is written as آ, always pronounced /a/, like a in father. آ is an initial letter which never joins the preceding or following letters.

Medial and final is written as ا, still with the sound /a/. It only joins the preceding letters for /a. e. o/

How to write it? Trace and practice below:

.... ا - ا - ا - ا - ا - ا - ا - ....ا....

.... ـا - ـا - ـا - ـا - ـا - ـا - ـا - ....ـا....

.... آ - آ - آ - آ - آ - آ - آ - ....آ....

....

---
www.persianbell.com

بـ ب

Letter be:

Short forms are initial parts of the full forms, and each letter has the first sound of its name:

Short form: بـ   full form: ب

Sound: /b/   name: /be/

In general, short letter take the initial and medial position of a syllable; full letters come only at the end:

Water: /âb/   آ + ب   آب

Dad: /bâbâ/   بـ + ا + بـ + ا   بابا

How to write it? Trace and practice below:

................بـ - بـ - بـ - بـ - بـ - بـ - بـ........

................ب - ب - ب - ب - ب - ب - ب........

................بـ - بـ - بـ - بـ - بـ - بـ........

................ب - ب - ب - ب - ب - ب........

www.persianbell.com

با - با - با ....

بابا - بابا - بابا ....

آب - آب - آب ....

New Words:

با - /bâ/ with

بابا - /bâbâ/ Father

آب - /âb/ water

د

Letter dal:

Letter د /dal/ has the sound /d/, like d in day

It only joins the preceding letter. persian /d/ is dental

Courtesy: /adab/ اَ + دَ + ب اَدَب

Bad: /bad/ بـ + ـد بد

How to write it? Trace and practice below:

د- د- د- د- د- د- د- د ....

د- د- د- د- د- د- د- د ....

باد- باد- باد- باد- باد ....

آباد- آباد- آباد- آباد- آباد ....

بابا آب داد.

Father gave water /bâbâ âb dâd/

....

باب با ادب آب داد.

Bob gives water politely/Bob bâ adab âb dâd/

....

New Words:

باد -/bâd/wind

آباد -/âbâd/ build

اَدب – adab/literature, politeness

....

....

....

....

....

....

ن ـنـ

Letter nun:

Letter ن ـنـ /nun/ has the sound /n/, like n in no

Bread /nān/  ن + ـا + ن   نان

Pure /nab/ ن + ـا + ب   ناب

How to write it? Trace and practice below:

نـ - ـنـ - ـنـ - ـنـ - ـنـ - ـنـ - ـنـ

ـن - ـن - ـن - ـن - ـن - ـن

ن - ن - ن - ن - ن - ن - ن

ن - ن - ن - ن - ن - ن - ن

ندا - ندا - ندا

بند - بند - بند

بن- بُن- بُن ....

دندان- دندان- دندان ....

ندا دندان ندارد.
Neda has no teeth/Bândâ dandân nadârad/
....

بابا نان داد. Father gave him/her bread/bâbâ nân dad/

....

New Words:

آن /ân/ it

بند /Band/ sling

بُن /bon/ root

دندان /dandân/ tooth

بدن /badan/ body

....
....

www.persianbell.com

ر

Letter re:

Letter ر /re/ has the sound /r/, like r in ray.

It only joins the preceding letter:

Flour: /ard/   آ + ر + د   آرد

Cloud: /abr/   اَ + بـ + ـر   ابر

How to write it? Trace and practice below:

ر ـ ر ـ ر ـ ر ـ ر ـ ر ....

ر ـ ر ـ ر ـ ر ـ ر ـ ر ....

برادر ـ برادر ـ برادر ....

باران ـ باران ـ باران ....

آن باربر بار دارد.

This carrier has a load /ân bârbar bâr dârad/

....

دارا برادر دارد.

Dara has a brother/Dârâ barâdar dârad/

....

New Words:

برادر /brother/barâdar

باران /rain/bârân

بردن /win, carry/bordan

دَر /door/dar

دُر /pearl /dor/

....

....

....

م ‍ـم

Letter mim:

Letter م ‍ـم /mim/ has the sound /m/, like m in man

Pencil: /medad/ ‍ـم + ا + د + د مداد

Almond: /badam/ 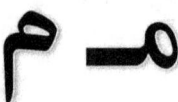 م + ا + د + ا + ب بادام

How to write it? Trace and practice below:

..ـم.. - ـم - ـم - ـم - ـم - ـم..........................

..ـمـ.. - ـمـ - ـمـ - ـمـ - ـمـ - ـمـ..........................

..مـ.. - مـ - مـ - مـ - مـ - مـ..........................

..م.. - م - م - م - م - م..........................

مادر - مادر - مادر ....

www.persianbell.com

تمام - تمام- تمام ....

بم- بم- بم ....

آرام- آرام- آرام- آرام ....

مادر بادام دارد.

Mother has almond /mâdar bâdâm dâd/

....

مراد در باران آمد.

Morad came in the rain/Morâd dar bârân âmad/

....

New Words:

مادر /mother/mâdar

تمام /finish / tamâm

بم /bass/Bam

آرام /slow/ârâm

مرد /man/mard

س ـس

Letter sin:

Letter /sin/ has the sound /s/, like s in sun س ـس

Basket: /sabad/   س + بـ + ـد   سَبد

Hourse: /asb/   اَ + سـ + ـب   اَسب

How to write it? Trace and practice below:

ســ - ســ - ســ - ســ - ســ - ســ ....

س - س - س - س - س - س ....

ـسی - ـسی - ـسی - ـسی - ـسی - ـسی ....

ـسی - ـسی - ـسی - ـسی - ـسی - ـسی ....

www.persianbell.com

سم- سم- سم ....

سمسار- سمسار- سمسار ....

آدامس- آدامس- آدامس ....

داس - داس- داس ....

اسما با اسب آمد.
Asma came with the horse/Asmâ bâ asb âmad/
....

سما داس در سبد دارد.
Sâmâ dâs dar sabad dârad

Sama has scythe in the basket
....

New Words:

سم /Sam/ poison

سمسار /semsâr/ dealer in second

آدامس /âdâms/ chewing gum

داس /dâs/ scythe

سن /sen/ age

www.persianbell.com

ت ـ ت

Letter te:

Letter /te/ has the sound /t/, like t in time ت ـ ت

Persian /t/ is dental

Fever: /tab/ تَ + ب تَب

Darts: /dārt/ د + ا + ر + ت دارت

How to write it? Trace and practice below:

ت ـ ت ـ ت ـ ت ـ ت ـ ت ـ ت ....

ـتـ ـ ـتـ ـ ـتـ ـ ـتـ ـ ـتـ ـ ـتـ ....

ـت ـ ـت ـ ـت ـ ـت ـ ـت ـ ـت ....

ت ـ ت ـ ت ـ ت ـ ت ـ ت ـ ت ....

تاب ـ تاب ـ تاب ـ تاب ـ تاب ....

www.persianbell.com

تبار- تبار- تَبار- تَبار- تَبار ....

دست - دست - دست- دست- دست ....

مات - مات - مات - مات- مات- مات ....

سارا تاب را بست.
Sara fasten the swing/ Sârâ tab ra bast/
....

برات ماست دارد.
Barat has yogurt/Bârât mâst dârad/
....

New Words:

تاب /swing/ tâb

تبار /ancestry/tabâr

دست /hand/dast

مات /aghast, opaque/ mât

ترس /fear/tars

ارادت /devotion/eradat

و

Letter vav:

Letter و /vāv/ has the sound /v, o, u/ it only Joins the preceding letter.

/v/ like v in very: bath /vān/   و + ا + ن   وان

/u/ like oo in too: river /rud/   ب + ـو + د   بود

/o/ like o in french mode: two /do/   د + و   دو

How to write it? Trace and practice below:

و- ـو- ـو- ـو- ـو- ـو- و- ـو...............................

و- و- و- و- و- و- و...............................

توت- توت- توت...............................

دوات- دوات- دوات...............................

داوود دوست اسد است.

Dawood is Assad's friend/Dâvud doost-e Asad ast/

....

نانوا نان را از تنور بیرون می آورد.

The baker took the bread out of the oven/nânvâ nân râ az tanoor biroon miâvard/

....

New Words:

توت /toot/ berry

داور /dâvar/ referee

دوات /Davât/ inkwell

توانا /Tavânâ/ able

رود /rud/ river

تو /to/ you (singular)

....

....

....

یـ ی

Letter ye:

Letter یـ ی /ye/ has the sound /y, i/

/y/ like y in yes interrogative particle /aya/

/i/ like ea in east:

Apple: /sib/   سـ + یـ + ب   سیب

Esophagus: /meri/   مـ + ـر + ی   مری

How to write it? Trace and practice below:

یـ - یـ - یـ - یـ - یـ - یـ

یـ - یـ - یـ - یـ - یـ - یـ

ی - ی - ی - ی - ی - ی

ی - ی - ی - ی - ی - ی

www.persianbell.com

یار - یار - یار ....

متین - متین - متین ....

سینی - سینی - سینی ....

دی - دی - دی ....

ماری سینی در دست دارد.

Mary has tray in her hand /Mari sini dar dast dârad/
....

یاسین میز درست می کند.

Yasin makes the table /Yasin miz dorost mikonad/
....

New Words:

یار /yâr/ alter ego, sweetheart, friend,

ریاست /riâst/ chairmanship

بینی /bini/ nose

بادی /bâdi/ windy

ز

Letter ze:

Letter ز /ze/ has the sound /z/, like z in zoo

It only joins the preceeding letter:

Green: / sabz/   ‌س + ب + ـز   سبز

Freedom: /azadi/   آ + ز + ا + د + ی   آزادی

How to write it? Trace and practice below:

ز - ژ - ژ - ژ - ژ - ژ - ژ ....

ز - ژ - ژ - ژ - ژ - ژ ....

بز - بژ - بژ - ....

زن - ژن - ژن - ....

ارز - ارژ - ارژ ....

آن زن با سوزن دامن می دوزد.

That woman sews the skirt with a needle /ân zan bâ soozan dâman midoozad/

....

دامن زینب تمیز بود.

Zeinab's skirt was clean /dâman-e Zeynab tamiz bood/

....

New Words:

بز /boz/ goat

ارز /arz/ currency

زیبا /zibâ/ beautiful

دزد /dozd/ thief

راز /râz/ mystery

....

....

ک ک

Letter kaf:

Letter ک ک /kāf/ has the sound /k/, like c in car:

Book: /ketâb/ ک + ت + ا + ب کتاب

Perception: /dark/ د + ر + ک درک

Place: /makân/ م + ک + ا + ن مکان

How to write it? Trace and practice below:

ک ـ ک ـ ک ـ ک ـ ک ـ ک ـ ک

ک ـ ک ـ ک ـ ک ـ ک ـ ک

ک ـ ک ـ ک ـ ک ـ ک ـ ک ـ ک

ک ـ ک ـ ک ـ ک ـ ک ـ ک ـ ک

کباب ـ کباب ـ کباب

www.persianbell.com

نمکدان- نمکدان- نمکدان ....

کمک- کمک- کمک ....

کودک- کودک- کودک ....

کودک نمکدان در دست دارد.
The baby is having a saltshaker/koodak namakdân dar dast dârad/

....

کامران کباب دُرست می کُنَد.
Kamran makes kebab/Kâmrân kabâb dorost mikonad/

....

New Words:

کمک /help/ komak

کر /deaf /kar/

کر /Chor /kor/

کیک /cack / keyk/

کود /dung, fertilizer / kood/

پ ـپ

Letter pe:

Letter پ ـپ /pe/ has the sound /p/ like p in pen

Onion   /piyâz/   پ + ـی + ـا + ز   پیاز

Ball: /toop/   ت + ـو + پ   توپ

How to write it? Trace and practice below:

.... پ - پ - پ - پ - پ - پ

.... پ - پ - پ - پ - پ

.... ـپ - ـپ - ـپ - ـپ - ـپ - ـپ

.... ـپ - ـپ - ـپ - ـپ - ـپ - ـپ

.... پارک - پارک - پارک

.... سپاس - سپاس - سپاس

www.persianbell.com

پمپ - پمپ- پمپ ....

سوپ - سوپ- سوپ ....

پوپک در پارک توپ بازی می کند.
Poopak play with ball in the park/Poopak dar pârk toop bazi mikonad/

....

پروین سوپ پیاز درست می کند.
Parvin makes onion soup/Parvin soop-e piyâz dorost mikonad/

....

New Words:

پارک /pârk/ park

سپاس /sepâs/ thank

پمپ /pomp/ pump

سوپ /soop/ soup

پیام /payâm/ message

پسر /pesar/ boy

ه ه‍ ‍ه‍ ‍ه

Letter he:

Letter ‍ه ه /he/ has the sound /h, e, a/

Written in four ways.

Initial: plural suffix /hā/ ‍ه + ‍ا ها

Medial: wide /pahn/ پ + ‍ه‍ + ‍ن پَهن

Final joined: no /na/ ن + ‍ه نه

Final disjoined: moon /māh/ م + ‍ا + ه ماه

How to write it? Trace and practice below:

هارون- هارون- هارون ....

مهتاب- مهتاب- مهتاب ....

نامه- نامه- نامه ....

پرنده- پرنده- پرنده ....

هارون و بهاره سه روز اهواز بودند.
Haroon and Bahare were in ahvaz for three days/Hâroon va Bahare ce rooz dar ahvaz boodand/

....

به به! مهتاب همه جا را روشن کرد.
Bravo! Light of moon turned on everywhere/bah bah! Mahtâb hame jâ râ roshan kard/

....

New Words:

همه /hame/ all

بهشت /behesht/ paradise

راه /rah/ way

Letter shin:

Letter ش ـش / shin / has sound /sh/, like sh in she

Night: /shab/ شَ + ـب شَب

Mouse, rat: / moosh/ مـ + ـو + ش موش

How to write it? Trace and practice below:

..شِـ- شَـ- شَـ- شَـ- شَـ- شَـ- شَـ ....

..شـِ- شـِ - شـِ- شـِ- شـِ- شـِ- شـِ ....

..شِ- شِ- شِ- شِ- شِ- شِ- شِ ....

..شِ- شِ- شِ- شِ- شِ- شِ- شِ ....

شما- شما- شما ....

هشت- هشت- هشت ....

www.persianbell.com

آتش- آتش - آتش ....

موش - موش- موش ....

شادی کشک را در آش می ریزد.
Shâdi pours curd into pottage /Shâdi kashk râ dar âsh mirizad/

....

امین شربت می نوشد.
Amin drinks syrup /Amin sharbat minooshad/

....

New Words:

آتش /âtash/ fire

موش /moosh/ mouse, rat

هشت /hasht/ eight

تشک /toshak/ mattress

شما /shomâ/ you

شک /shak/ doubt

ف ـف

Letter fe:

Letter ف ف /fe/ has the sound /f/, like in food

Note book: /daftar/ د + فـ + ـتـ + ـر   دفتر

Navel: /nâf/ نـ + ـا + ف   ناف

How to write it? Trace and practice below:

ف ـ ف ـ ف ـ ف ـ ف ـ ف ....

ڤ ـ ڤ ـ ڤ ـ ڤ ـ ڤ ـ ڤ ....

ـف ـ ـف ـ ـف ـ ـف ـ ـف ـ ـف ....

ف ـ ف ـ ف ـ ف ـ ف ـ ف ....

فرش ـ فرش ـ فرش ....

www.persianbell.com

هفت - هفت - هفت ....

کیف - کیف - کیف ....

اشرف - اشرف - اشرف ....

اشرف فرش دستباف برای فروش دارد.

Ashraf has handmade carpet for sale/Ashraf farsh dastbâf barâye foroosh dârad

....

فردا هوا ابری است.

Tomorrow the weather is cloudy/Fardâ havâ abri ast.

....

New Words:

فرزند /farzand/ offspring

کفش /kafsh/ shoes

کیف /kif/ bag

کیف /keyf/ gratification, pleasure

شرف /sharaf/ honor

خ ـخ

Letter khe:

Letter ـخ خ /khe/ has the sound /kh/

Like ch in Scottish loch in german bach

Three: /derakht/ د + ر + ـخ + ـت درخت

Gules: /sorkh/ س + ـر + خ سرخ

How to write it? Trace and practice below:

ـخ - ـخ - ـخ - ـخ - ـخ - ـخ ..

ـخـ - ـخـ - ـخـ - ـخـ - ـخـ - ـخـ ..

خـ - خـ - خـ - خـ - خـ - خـ ..

خ - خ - خ - خ - خ - خ ..

خرما - خرما - خرما

تخته- تخته- تخته ....

میخ- میخ- میخ ....

سوراخ- سوراخ- سوراخ ....

خسرو برای خواهرش کتاب می خواند.
Khosrow reads a book for his sister /Khosrow barâye khâharash ketâb mikhânad/

....

نادر میخ و تخته دارد.
Nader has nail and lamber /Nader mikh va takhte dârad/

....

New Words:

خرما /khormâ/ date

تخته /takhteh/ lamber

سیخ /sikh/ skewer

خرس /sikh/ bear

سوراخ /soorâkh/ hole

خروس /khoroos/ rooster

چ

Letter che:

Letter چ چ /che/ has the sound /č/ like ch in china

Print: /chap/ چ + ا + پ چاپ

Migration: /kooch/ ک + و + چ کوچ

How to write it? Trace and practice below:

.... چ - چ - چ - چ - چ - چ .. چ

.... ـچـ - ـچـ - ـچـ - ـچـ - ـچـ .. ـچـ

.... ـج - ـج - ـج - ـج - ـج - ـج ... ـج

.... ج - ج - ج - ج - ج - ج ... ج

.... چوپان - چوپان - چوپان

پنچر - پنچر- پنچر ....

سوییچ - سوییچ - سوییچ - ....

پوچ - پوچ-پوچ - ....

چوپان بزها را به چراگاه برد.
Shepherd took the goats to the pasture/choopân bozhâ râ be charâgâh bord/

....

چهره اش زیبا است.
Her face is beautiful/Chehre-ash zibâ ast./

....

New Words:

چهره /face/chehreh

سوییچ /switch/suich

پوچ /Empty, Absurd /pooch

پنچر /puncture/panchar

قاچ /slice/ghâch

ق ـق

Letter ghaf:

Letter ق ق /ghaf/ has the sound /q/, like r in french rue. Persian /q/ is harder

Spoon: /qashoq/   ق + ـا + شُ + ـق   قاشق

Horn: /boogh/   بـ + ـو + ق   بوق

How to write it? Trace and practice below:

ق ـ ق ـ ق ـ ق ـ ق ـ ق ـ ق ....

ـقـ ـ ـقـ ـ ـقـ ـ ـقـ ـ ـقـ ـ ـقـ ـ ـقـ ....

ـق ـ ق ـ ق ـ ق ـ ق ـ ق ـ ق ....

ـق ـ ق ـ ق ـ ق ـ ق ـ ق ـ ق ....

قوری ـ قوری ـ قوری ....

منقار - منقار- منقار ....

هق هق – هق هق- هق هق ....

برق - برق- برق ....

قباد بشقاب و قاشق را آورد.
Ghobad brought a plate and spoon/Ghobâd boshghâb va ghâshogh râ âvard/

....

شفیق قندان را پر از قند کرد.
Shafiq filled the sugarcane with hard sugar. /Sahfiq ghandân râ por az ghand kard/

....

New Words:

قوری /teapot/ghoori

منقار /beak/menghâr

هق هق /sob/hegh-hegh

برق /electricity/bargh

قرمز /red/ghermez

قاب /frame/ghâb

گ ک

Leter gaf:

Letter ک گ /gāf/ has the sound /g/, like g in a garden

Dog: /sag/   س + ـگ   سگ

Wolf: /gorg/   گ + ـر + گ   گرگ

How to write it? Trace and practice below:

گ - گ - گ - گ - گ - گ - گ - گ ....

ـگ - ـگ - ـگ - ـگ - ـگ - ـگ - ـگ ....

ـگـ - ـگـ - ـگـ - ـگـ - ـگـ - ـگـ - ـگـ ....

ک - ک - ک - ک - ک - ک - ک - ک ....

گوش - گوش - گوش - ....

مگس - مگس - مگس - مگس - ....

دیگ - دیگ - دیگ - دیگ - ....

هاگ - هاگ - هاگ - هاگ - ....

گرگ به گوسفندان نزدیک می شود.
The wolf is approaching the sheep/gorg be goosfandân nazdik mishavad/

....

مگس روی دانش آموز نشست.
The fly sit on the student. /magas ruye dânesh âmuz neshast/

....

New Words:

گوش /goosh/ ear

مگس / magas/ fly

دیگ /dig/ cauldron, pot

هاگ /hâg/ spore

گردو /gerdoo/ walnut

ج ‍ج

Letter jim:

Letters ‍ج ج /jim/ has the sound j in just

Chicken: /juje/ 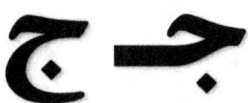 ه‍ + و + ج + ج   جوجه

Pine: /kâj/ ‍ج + ‍ا + ک   کاج

How to write it? Trace and practice below:

.... ج‍ - ج‍ - ج‍ - ج‍ - ج‍ - ج‍ ... ج‍ ...

.... ‍ج‍ - ‍ج‍ - ‍ج‍ - ‍ج‍ - ‍ج‍ - ‍ج‍ -.. ‍ج‍ ..

.... ‍ج - ‍ج - ‍ج - ‍ج - ‍ج - ‍ج ... ‍ج ..

.... ج - ج - ج - ج - ج - ج ... ج ..

.... جواهر - جواهر - جواهر

سنجاب - سنجاب - سنجاب ....

نارنج - نارنج - نارنج ....

موج - موج - موج ....

نسرین سه سنجاب روی درخت دید.
Nasrin saw three squirrels on the tree./Nasrin se sanjâb rooye derakht did/

....

جمشید درخت کاج خرید.
Jamshid purchased a pine tree./Jamshid derakht-e kaj kharid./

....

New Words:

جواهر /Jewel /Javâher/

نارنج /sour orange/nâranj/

سنجاب /squirrel/sanjâb/

موج /wave/mowj/

اوج /top, climax/owj/

ل ـل

Letter lam:

Letter ل ـل /lām/ has the sound /L/, like l in love

Flower: /gol/   گ ـ + ـل   گل

Wing: /bâl/   ب ـ + ـا + ل   بال

How to write it? Trace and practice below:

ل ـ ل ـ ل ـ ل ـ ل ـ ل ....

ل ـ ل ـ ل ـ ل ـ ل ـ ل ....

ـل ـ ـل ـ ـل ـ ـل ـ ـل ـ ـل ....

ل ـ ل ـ ل ـ ل ـ ل ـ ل ....

لیوان ـ لیوان ـ لیوان ....

کلاس ـ کلاس ـ کلاس ....

بلبل - بلبل - بلبل ....

جدال - جدال - جدال ....

جلیل گل در گلدان گذاشت.
Jalil put flower in the pot. /Jalil gol dar goldân gozâsht/

....

لیلا سلام کرد.
Leyla said hello /Leyla salâm kard/

....

New Words:

لیوان /livân/ glass

کلاس /kelâs/ class

بلبل /bolbol/ nightingale

جدال /Jedâl/ controversy

لباس /lebâs/ cloth

سلامتی /salâmati/ healthy, healthful

ژ

Letter zhe:

Letter ژ /zhe/ has the sound /ž/, like s in measure. It only joins the preceding letter:

Droopy:/pazhmordeh/ ه+د + ـر + ـم + ـژ + پـ پژمرده

Radiator: /shoofazh/ ژ + ـا + ف + ـو + شـ شوفاژ

How to write it? Trace and practice below:

......-ݰ-ژ-ژ-ژ-ژ-ژ-ژ

......-ژ-ژ-ژ-ژ-ژ-ژ-ژ

......پژو- پژو- پژو

......ژاپن- ژاپن- ژاپن

ژاله ژورنالیست است.

Zhaleh is a journalist/ Zhaleh zhurnâlist ast/

اگر به گل آب نرسد پژمرده می شود.

If the flower doesn't receive water, it will be wither / agar be gol âb naresad pazhmordeh mishavad.

New Words:

پژو /pezho/ Peugeot

ژاپن /zhâpon/ Japan

پژوهش /pazhuhesh/ research

پژواک /pezhvak/ eco

دژ /dezh/ fortress

ص ص

Leter sad:

Letter ص ص /sād/ has the sound /s/, like s in sun:

Special: /khas/   ص + ا + خ   خاص

Face: /soorat/   ص + و + ر + ت   صورت

How to write it? Trace and practice below:

صـ .. صـ - صـ- صـ- صـ- صـ- صـ ....

ـصـ .. ـصـ - ـصـ- ـصـ- ـصـ- ـصـ- ـصـ ....

ـص .. ـص - ـص- ـص- ـص- ـص- ـص ....

ص .. ص - ص- ص- ص- ص- ص ....

صابون - صابون- صابون ....

شصت - شصت- شصت- ....

www.persianbell.com

مخلص - مخلص - مخلص ....

مخصوص - مخصوص - مخصوص ....

ناصر صورت خود را با صابون شست.
Naser washed his faces with soap/Nâser soorat khod râ bâ sâboon shost/

....

من صندلی مخصوص دارم.
I have a special chair/man sandeli-ye makhsoos dâram/

....

New Words:

شصت /sixty/shast

مخلص /sincere/mokhles

صد /hundred/sad

مخصوص /special/makhsus

مصدر /infinitive/masdar

خالص /pure/khâles

ح ـح

Letter he:

Letter ح ـح /he/ has the sound /h/, like h in he

Location: /mahal/   م + ح + ل   محل

Ghost: /rooh/   ر + و + ح   روح

How to write it? Trace and practice below:

ح ـ ح ـ ح ـ ح ـ ح ـ ح ....

ح ـ ح ـ ح ـ ح ـ ح ـ ح ....

ج ـ ج ـ ج ـ ج ـ ج ـ ج ....

ح ـ ح ـ ح ـ ح ـ ح ـ ح ....

حوله ـ حوله ـ حوله ....

صبحانه ـ صبحانه ـ صبحانه ....

www.persianbell.com

صبح - صبح- صبح ....

لوح- لوح- لوح ....

ساناز هر روز صبحانه می خورد.
Sanaz eats breakfast everyday /Sânâz har rooz sobhâneh mikhorad/

....

مصباح دست و صورت خود را با حوله خشک می کند.
Mesbah dries hands and face with a towel/Mesbâh dast va soorate khod râ bâ holeh khoshk mikonad/

....

New Words:

حوله /holeh/ towel

صبح /sobh/ morning

لوح /loh/ tablet, table

صحیح /sahih/ correct

لایحه /lâyehe/ bill (draft law)

محل /mahal/ location

www.persianbell.com

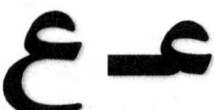

Letter eyn:

Letter ع ـع /eyn/ has the sound /?, like a slight cough.

As in cockney bottle /eyn/ is written in four ways.

Initial: number /?adad/   عـ + ـد + د   عدد

Medial: teacher /sh?r/   شـ + ـعـ + ر   شعر

Final joined: a quarter /rob?/   ر + بـ + ـع   ربع

Final disjoined: start /shoro?/   شـ + ر + و + ع   شروع

How to write it? Trace and practice below:

عقربه - عقربه- عقربه ....

جعفری - جعفری- جعفری ....

جمع - جمع- جمع ....

شجاع - شجاع- شجاع ....

پسر شجاع به او کمک کرد.
A brave boy helps him (her)/pesare shojâ' be ou komak kard/

....

جعفر موقع ظهر بچه ها را در یک جا جمع کرد.
Ja'far gathered the children in a place at noon/Jafar moghe' zohr bachehâ râ dar yekjâ jam' kard.

....

New Words:

عقربه /aqrabeh/ pointer

معده /me'deh/ stomach

جمع /jam'/ addition

جعفری /ja'fari/ parsley

ث ـث

Letter se:

Letter ث ـث /se/ has the sound /s/, like s in sun

Discussion: /bahs/   ب + ـح + ـث   بحث

Inheritance: /ers/   ا + ر + ث   ارث

How to write it? Trace and practice below:

ثـ - ثـ - ثـ - ثـ - ثـ - ثـ ....

ـثـ - ـثـ - ـثـ - ـثـ - ـثـ - ـثـ ....

ـث - ـث - ـث - ـث - ـث - ـث ....

ث - ث - ث - ث - ث - ث ....

ثریا - ثریا - ثریا ....

مثل - مثل - مثل ....

باعث- باعث- باعث ....

وارث- وارث- وارث ....

لثه کثیف باعث بیماری می شود.
Dirty gum causes disease/lase kasif ba'es-e bimari mishavad/

....

بحث سیاسی ممنوع است.
Political discussion is prohibited/Bahs-e siasi mamnoo' ast./

....

New Words:

ثابت /sâbet/ constant, stable

مثل /mesl/ like

مثل /masal/ proverb

باعث /bâes/ cause

وارث /Vâres/ heir

مثبت /mosbat/ positive

Letter zad:

Letter ض ضـ /zād/ has the sound /z/, like z in zoo

Present: /hâzer/   حـ + ـا + ضـ + ـر   حاضر

Disease: /maraz/   مـ + ـر + ض   مرض

How to write it? Trace and practice below:

ص ـ ضـ ـ ضـ ـ ضـ ـ ضـ ـ ضـ ـ ضـ

ضـ ـ ضـ ـ ضـ ـ ضـ ـ ضـ ـ ضـ

ـض ـ ض ـ ـض ـ ـض ـ ـض ـ ـض

ض ـ ض ـ ض ـ ض ـ ض ـ ض

ضعیف ـ ضعیف ـ ضعیف

افضل - افضل - افضل ....

ریاضی - ریاضی - ریاضی ....

حوض - حوض - حوض ....

راضیه در درس ریاضی ضعیف است.
Razieh is poor in the math lesson/Râziyeh dar darse riâzi zae'if ast./

....

آنها در حوض آب بازی می کنند.
They play in the pool/Anha dar howz-e âb bâzi mikonand./

....

New Words:

ضعیف /za'if/ poor, weak

افضل /afzal/ better

ریاضی /riâzi/ math

حوض /howz/ small pool, tub

Letter gheyn:

Letter غـ غ /ghyn/ has the sound /q/, like r in french rue.

Persian /q/ is harder. /gheyn/ is written in four ways:

Initial: goose/ghaz/ غـ + ا + ز غاز

Medial: owl/joghd/ جـ + ـغـ + ـد جغد

Final joind: blade/tigh/ تـ + ـيـ + ـغ تیغ

Final disjoined: garden/ bagh/ بـ + ا + غ باغ

How to write it? Trace and practice below:

غار - غار - غار ....

شغل - شغل - شغل ....

مبلغ - مبلغ - مبلغ ....

باغ - باغ - باغ ....

باغبان در باغ خود شلغم کاشت.
The gardener planted turnip in his garden/bâgheban dar bâgh-e khod shalgham kâsht./

....

غیاث مبلغی پول از دوستش گرفت.
Qias took money from his friend/Ghiâs mablaghi pool az doostah gereft./

....

New Words:

غار /cave/ghâr

شغل /job/shoghl

مبلغ /amount/ mablagh

باغ /garden/bâgh

غمگین /sad/ghamgin

نابغه /genius/nâbegheh

www.persianbell.com

ط

Letter ta:

Letter ط /ta/ has the sound /t/, like t in top

Rope: /tanâb/   ط ‍ + ‍نـ + ‍ا + ب   طناب

Yard: /hayât/   حـ + ‍يـ + ‍ا + ط   حياط

How to write it? Trace and practice below:

ط ‍- ط ‍- ط ‍- ط ‍- ط ‍- ط ‍- ط ....

ـط ‍- ـط ‍- ـط ‍- ـط ‍- ـط - ـط ‍- ـط ....

ـطـ ‍- ـطـ ‍- ـطـ ‍- ـطـ ‍- ـطـ - ـطـ ‍- ـطـ ....

ط - ط - ط - ط - ط - ط - ط ....

باطل - باطل - باطل ....

مطب - مطب - مطب ....

www.persianbell.com

وسط - وسط- وسط ....

نشاط - نشاط- نشاط ....

طبیب بیمار را مداوا کرد.
A doctor medicates the patient. /tabib bimar râ modâvâ kard/

....

جمعه تعطیل است.
Friday is holiday. /Jom'e tatil ast./

....

New Words:

باطل /bâtel/ void

مطب /matab/ doctor's office (clinic)

وسط /vasat/ center

نشاط /neshât/ cheerfulness

طلا /talâ/ gold

مطلب /matlab/ content, subject

این طور /in-towr/ like this way

Letter za:

Letter ظ /za/ has the sound /z, like z in ziro.

Suspicios: /zan/   ظ + ن   ظن

Order: /nazm/   ن + ظ + م   نظم

How to write it? Trace and practice below:

ظ - ظ - ظ - ظ - ظ - ظ - ظ ....

ظ - ظ - ظ - ظ - ظ - ظ ....

ظ - ظ - ظ - ظ - ظ - ظ ....

ظ - ظ - ظ - ظ - ظ - ظ ....

ظریف - ظریف - ظریف ....

تظاهر - تظاهر - تظاهر ....

غلیظ - غلیظ - غلیظ ....

حفاظ - حفاظ - حفاظ ....

حافظ معروفترین شاعر زبان فارسی است.
Hafiz is the most famous poet in the Persian language.
/Hâfez ma'ruftarin shâ'er zabâne fârsi ast./

....

رعایت نظم و انضباط از اصول اولیه هر کاری است.
Discipline is one of the basic principles of any work.
/ra'âyat naz va enzebât az osule avaliyeh har kâri ast./

....

New Words:

ظریف /zarif/ delicate

تظاهر /tazâhor/ pretense

مظلوم /mazlum/ Oppressed

غلیظ /ghaliz/ dense

لحاظ کردن /lahâz kardan/ to include, considering

حفاظ /hefâz/ shield

ذ

Letter zal:

Letter ذ /zal/ has the sound /z/, like z in zoom

It only joins the preceding letter:

Delicious: /laziz/	لـ + ـذ + يـ + ـذ	لذيذ

Verve: /zowgh/	ذ + و + ق	ذوق

How to write it? Trace and practice below:

ـذ - ـذ - ـذ - ـذ - ـذ - ـذ - ـذ ....

ذ - ذ - ذ - ذ - ذ - ذ - ذ ....

بذل - بذل - بذل ....

ذخيره - ذخيره - ذخيره ....

اذان - اذان - اذان ....

آبگوشت غذای لذیذی است.
Broth is a delicious food. /âbgoosht ghazây-e lazizi ast/

....

مورچه ها برای زمستان آذوقه ذخیره می کنند.
Ants provision food for their winter./Moorchehâ barâye zemstâne âzoogheh zakhireh mikonand/

....

New Words:

بذل /munificence/bazl/

ذخیره /store/ zakhireh/

اذان /call to prayer, Azan /azân/

کذب /false, lie/kezb/

رذل /scoundrel/razl/

گذشت /forgiveness, pardon/gozasht/

....

....

ء

Letter ham-ze:

Letter ء /hamze/ has the sound /?/, This Arabic sign is a "glottal stop" like between the syllsbles of "uh-oh".

ء is written likes these forms:

$$ ء - أ - إ - ؤ - ؤَ - ئُ - ئ - ة $$

| امضاء   ا + مـ + ـضـ + ـا + ء | Sign: /emza?/ |

| پائین   پـ + ـا + ئ + ـیـ + ـن | Down: /pa?in/ |

How to write it? Trace and practice below:

 ء - ء - ء - ء - ء - ء ....

نئون - نئُون - نئُون - ....

مؤدب - مؤَدب - مؤَدب - ....

www.persianbell.com

شیء - شیء- شیء- شیء ....

تلألو- تلألو- تلألو- تلألو ....

سؤالی نداری؟
Do you have any questions? /So?âli nadari?/
....

رئیس اداره در مأموریت است.
The head of the department is on a mission /Ra?is edâreh dar ma'mooriat ast/
....

New Words:

جزء component /Joz?/

شیء object /shey?/

نئون neon /ne?on/

مؤدب polite /mo?adab/

تلألؤ glint /tala?lo?/

مؤثر effective /mo?as-ser/

مستأجر tenant /mosta?jer/

Learn Like a Native

مثل زبان مادری

یاد بگیریم

Practice Like a Native

Vowels:

Persian vowels-pesian has six simple vowels:

Short vowels   a as in English hat, animal

Short vowels   e as in English men, element

Short vowels   o as in French mode, ocean

Long vowels   ā as in English father, arm

Long vowels   i as in English east, need

Long vowels   u as in English zoo, too

Tere are also several vowel combination, like /ow/and/ey/, each consisting of a vowel and a consonant. The younger generation use a simple /o/, or a slighty longer /o/, as a subtitute for/ow/. The sign/ow/ is used after the words involving this sound in wordlists and dictionaries of this book.

Vowels at the beginnigs- short vowels are initially written with alef and the signs ─,─,─, which stand respectively for /a,e,o/. They are placed above or below alef:

/om/ اُم   /em/ اِم   /am/ اَم

Vowel signs are not usually used in writing except at elementary stages of learning or to avoid ambiguities. Alef in also used for writing initial long vowels:

That,it   /ān/   آن

this   /in/   این

that,he,she, it   /un/   اون

Vowel in the middel:

short vowels \a,e,o\ are not usually written in the middle of a syllable. when necessary, they are represented by the sign ◌َ,◌ِ,◌ُ, which are placed above or below the previous letters:

I:	\man\	مَن
Yen:	\yen\	یِن
Ton:	\ton\	تُن

Long vowels \ā,i,u\ are written with the letters الف، ی and و:

Bread:	\nān\	نان
Team:	\tim\	تیم
Feast:	\sur\	سور

Vowels at the end:

a	نَه	/na/	no
e	بِه	/be/	to
o	تُو	/to/	you(sing)
ā	ما	/ma/	we
i	چی	/ci/	what
u	تو	/tu/	in, inside

و/o/ is distinguished form و/u/ by the sign ◌ُ:

| You (sign) | /to/ | تُو |
| In, inside | /tu/ | تو |

Multiphones letters

Multiphonous letters (حروف چند صدا): Among the 33 persian letters, الف, ه, و and ی are pronounced in more than one way; each of the remaining 29 letters has a single sound.

Persian words consist of one or more syllables up to about eight. Be careful to give each syllable its full value and not to clip the words as it is often the tendency in English.

In the absence of phonetic spelling, the pronunciation of multiphonous letters is made simple with vowel signs as used in the present book:

الف /ā,a,e,o/

Is (ast) /a/ اَست   that,it (ân) /ā/ آن

Professor (oatâd) /o/ اُستاد   name (nâm) /e/ اِسم

و /v,u,o,ow/

Far (dur) /u/ دور   time (vaght) /v/ وَقت

New (no) /o/ یا /ow/ نُو   two (do) /o/ دو

ه /h,e,a/

Three (se) /e/ سه   also (ham) /h/ هَم

(Final /a/ is frequent in speech)   no (na) /a/ نَه

ی /y,i,ey/	
یا or (yâ) /y/	کی Who (ki) /i/
	کِی When (key) /ey/

Same pronunciation

Persian alphabet with same pronunciation:

ت - ة ط	T like the "t" in tree
ق - ﻕ غ - ـغ - ـغـ - غـ	Gh like "r" in French word 'Merci'
ه - ـه - ـهـ - هـ ح - ﺣ	H like "h" in 'Home'
ث - ﺛ س - ﺳ ص - ﺻ	S like "s" in 'Sun'
ذ ز ض - ﺿ ظ	Z like the "z" in 'Zoo'

Arabic Leters:

Regarding the alphabet which is an adoption from arabic with addition of four persian letters, we have placed it at the end of the book, with a clear pronunciation for each letter, to facilitate the learning as the reader may know, in persian there are several letters which don't exist in english. In order to provide sounds more or less the same, there have been combinations between two letters, which together could bring about the sound of a letter that exists in persian. Here are the examples:

Gh- A seraping gutteral sound, something similar to gurgling in the way french people pronounce letter r in words such as paris, merci, etc.

Kh- A strong sound from the back of the throat like german ch in word achtung (attention) or letter j in spanish like juan or simply as kh in khomeini.

Zh- A very soft sound as in english words measure, leisure, of french word je (I) or persian word zhale meaning dew (also name of a girl).

Q- A strong voice like in Quarantine or Qur'an (the holy book of islam).

Initial hamze:

All persian vowels at the initial position are preceded by hamze. when they are pronounced clearly and emphatically. The following words, for instance, begin with hamze in an emphatic situation:

Is:	\ʔast\	اَست
Name:	\ʔesm\	اِسم
Room:	\ʔoˈtāq\	اُتاق
Man, sir, mr:	\ʔāˈghā\	آقا
Iran:	\irān\	ایران
That, he, she, it	\ʔun\	اون

Initial hamze is normally omitted or weekened in speech and its disuse does not create any problem in communication. Thus, we have disregarded its usage in phonetic spelling for the sake of facility and ease of learning.

"ا" of "است" is removed after vowels in reading and sometimes in writing.

او دانشجو است ⟵ او دانشجوست

Joined form of "to be": Joined forms of بودن are formed by adding to be endings to nouns, adjectives, or pronouns. They occur very frequently both in the formal and informal language, especially in speech:

خوب هستم = خوبم   خوب هستیم = خوبیم

To be endings take ی or ا after vowels:

رها هستم = رهایم؛ افغانی هستیم = افغانی ایم؛ دانشجو هستید = دانشجویید

Tanvin

"ً" is called "tanvin" (in Arabic "Tanwiin") and is a grammatical suffix (an "attachment" to the end of the word). Tanvin sounds "an" and it always comes at the end of Arabic words that are used in Persian.

قطعاً /ghatan/: certainly

مَثَلاً /masalan/: for example

دَقیقاً /daghighan/: exactly

Tashdid

The orthographic sign " ّ " indicated the doublling of a consonant in pronunciation with out the releasing the consonant:

Thank you \moteshak-keram\   مُتِشَکّرم   مُتِشَک + کرم

Carpenter \naj-jâr\   نجّار   نجـ + جار

Painter \nagh-ghâsh\   نقّاش   نقـ + قاش

Genitive

Genitive introduced as اضافه ("ezâfe") that marks a relationship between two or more words. Most of the relationships like preposition "of" in English. It shows belonging to something or someone, possessiveness. Also, adjectives are related to the noun or noun phrase they modify using the genitive case. The ezafe (literally addition) is a very common structure formed of an unstressed /e/ (sounds as "e" in "men") between a noun or other part of speech and modifying elements which follow. The structure may consist of several words.

His book: \ketab-e ou\   کتابِ او

Genitive after vowels: As a rule, two successive vowels are separated by the mediatory consonant ی.

دانِشجویِ زَبانِ فارسی /dâneshjuye zabân-e fârsi/

The student of Persian language

To resolve vowel hiatus, "e" becomes "ye" ("ی") after vowels.

Hamze: Hamze is used as genetive and pronunce like short vovel "e".

My home: \khaneye man\   خانهٔ ما (خانه ی ما)

In Persian script, short vowels including "e", are not normally written. As a result, the genitive marker does not appear in writing unless it is pronounced "ye".

Gender

It does not distinguish between masculine, feminine or neuter genders. The fact of being male or female is expressed lexically rather than grammatically. There is no grammatical gender in Farsi.

The example indicate the subject could be either gender.

دوست او دانشجو ست.

His/her friend is student. /doost-e ou dâneshjoost/

Regarding nouns that do not have different words for male and female human beings, the words مرد /mard/ (man), زن /zan/ (woman), پسر /pesar/ (boy), دختر /dokhtar/ (girl), can be used to indicate their gender.

دانشجوی پسر boy student /daneshjoo-ye pesar/

دانشجوی دختر girl student /daneshjoo-ye dokhtar/

Regarding animal nouns that do not have different words for male and female, the adjectives نر /nar/ (male) and ماده mâdde (female) are used to indicate their gender:

شیر نر / shir-e nar / lion

شیر ماده / shir-e mâdde / lioness

Accusative case

The postposition را ("râ") marks the accusative case and indicates the object of the verb. "را" follows a noun or phrase which is used as the object of a verb, and the object is definite and specific.

"را" /râ/ is always used after objects. Therefore, it is considered an object marker.

دوستم کتاب را خرید.
My friend purchased book /Dustam ketâb râ kharid/

برادرش را دیدم /barâdar-ash râ didam/ I saw his brother.

Conjunction

Conjunctions link two words, phrases, or sentences together. The following are examples of simple conjunctions:

و، یا، هم، اگر، امّا، تا، چون

The Conjunction و : /va/ between sentences, phrases and within phrases in the formal style. also, /o/ in speech (occasionally omittable), and /o/ with the phrase in the formal style.

Sometimes, "تا" is used as a conjunction, meaning "in order to" or "to".

The counting unit تا: It used as a counting unit following چند and numerals (except یک and یکی). It may refer both to things and person in the spoken language:

چند تا بچّه داره؟ یکی داره. سه تا داره

Also, تا is used as a preposition for time "till", place "as far as, to "and counting "to":

از مدرسه تا بازار   از ساعت هشت تا ساعت ده   از دو تا دوازده

Sometimes "که" is used as a conjunction, meaning who, where, which, and that.

You can find the most common conjunctions in the following table

And	/va/	وَ
Or	/yâ/	یا
But	/agar/	اَگَر
Because	/chon/	چون
But	/ammâ/	اَما
But	/vali/	وَلی
Also	/ham/	هَم
Till/Until	/tâ/	تا
Which/That	/ke/	که

Interrogative

In Persian, the interrogative and indicative sentences are constructed the same. It is only through the intonation and articulation that the listener recognizes a sentence as being an indicative or interrogative.

In the *indicative*, the tone falls at the end of the sentence, while in the *interrogative*, it rises. If one of the interrogative pronouns (who, what, when, where, why, which, how) is present, it takes the stress, and, like the indicative, the voice inflection falls at the end of the sentence.

In formal Persian (and occasionally in colloquial Persian) sometimes an interrogative sentence begins with the interrogative particle آیا /ayâ/. The syntactic function of آیا /ayâ/ is very close the "tell me" In the sentence, which is a sentence opener that prepares the listener for a question to be posed.

To sum up, an interrogative sentence may be indicated by (1) the intonation, (2) by the prepositional particle آیا, or (3) by using one of the interrogative pronouns:

The interrogative " آیا " is used more in writing to make questions.

In speech, " آیا " is removed and the interrogative is indicated by the rising intonation.

غذا را خوردی.

Indicative: You ate the food. /ghazā rā khordi/

غذا را خوردی؟

Interrogative: Did you eat the food?/ ghazā rā khordi?/

آیا غذا را خوردی؟

Interrogative: Did you eat the food?/āyā ghazā rā khordi?/

کِی غذا را خوردی؟

Interrogative: When did you eat the food? /Key ghazā rā khordi?/

In the last sentence, the interrogative pronoun takes the stress, and, like the indicative, the voice inflection falls at the end of the sentence, while it rises in the other two interrogative sentences.

Plural of Nouns

Plural of nouns: ان /ān/ is the plural Persian suffix for animates in the formal and literary language. ان takes the mediatory consonant ی after the vowels /ā/ and /u/. ها is the plural Persian suffix for animates. It is also used for animates instead of ان as less formal suffix. Some animate takes only ها for the plural.

The formation of plural in Persian, can be divided into four categories:

- Using the plural suffix "ها" (-hâ)
- Using the plural suffix "ان" (-ân)
  If word ended with vowel, we add "ی".
- Arabic plural forms "ات" (-ân)
- Irregular

Singular: **Plural:**

Book/ketâb/ کتاب   Books/ketâbhâ/ کتابها

Man/mard/ مرد   Men/mardân/ مردان

Wise/dânâ/ دانا (vowel)   Wises/dânâyân/ دانایان

Word/kalame/ کلمه   Words/kalamât/ کلمات

Sense/hes/ حس (Irreg.)   Senses/havâs/ حواس

Conjugation

Verb Conjugation is the process of changing the verbs based on who is doing the action and when.

In English we add -ed to regular verbs for the past tense: "I work" becomes "I worked." We also add -s or -es to in the singular third person: "I run," becomes "she runs.", "I go" becomes "she goes".

In Persian conjugating verbs follow regular patterns according to three factors:

1. **Person** – verb conjugations are different depending on the pronoun (the person who is doing the action), i.e., depending on whether I, you, he (or she), etc.

2. **Number** – singular (for one person) or plural (for more than one person) – thus conjugations different depending on if it is او (u) – 'he/she' or آنها (ânhâ) – 'they'.

3. **Tense** – in Persian, we have past ("goftam" گفتم – "I said"); present ("miguyam" می گویم – "I say"); and future ("khâham goft" – خواهم گفت - "I will say").

To conjugate a verb, you need to use verbal endings for each pronoun.

Verbal Endings:

There are five past Verbal Endings for six personal pronouns (for third person, there is no verbal ending):

م ، ی ، ...- یم ، ید، ند

	Singular			Plural		
First Person	رفتم	م	من /I/man	رفتیم	یم	ما/We/mâ
Second Person	رفتی	ی	تو /You/to	رفتید	ید	شما/You/shomâ
Third Person	رفت	-	او He, She/u/	رفتند	ند	آنها – ایشان /They /ânhâ- ishan/

Convert letters:

تبدیل حروف: حروف قریب المخرج در معدودی از کلمات به یکدیگر تبدیل می شوند. از آن جمله همزه به (ه) مانند است: هست، است:هسته

(**ب**) به (**و**) مانند آب: آو – باز: واز – برداشت: ورداشت – شب: شو – سبز: سوز

(**ت**) به (**د**) مانندتشک: دشک – توت: تود – کتخدا: کدخدا

(**ج**) به (**ژ**) مانند باج: باژ – کج: کژ

(**ذ**) به (**د**) گذار: گدار – گنبذ: گنبد – موبذ: موبد

(**ف**) به (**پ**) مانند فارس: پارس – فیل: پیل

(**گ**) در پایان واژه پهلوی به (ه) ناملفوظ در فارسی دری، مانند خستگ: خسته، زندگ: زنده، ستارگ: ستاره، مژدگ: مژده، یاوگ:یاوه

یادآوری: کلمات (به آن، به این، به او) غالبا به صورت (بدان، بدین، بدو) در می آیند.

(ن، ب): هر گاه در میان کلمه ای "ن" قبل از "ب" واقع گردد میم تلفظ می شود ولی در نوشتن همان نون نوشته می شود: شنبه، انبر، انبان، سنبه. و چون در آخر کلمه باشد در نوشتن نیز تبدیل به م می گردد: دم، خم، سم که در اصل دنب، خنب، سنب بوده است.

Vav

واو معدوله: واوی است که در تعدادی از کلمات پس از حرف (خ) قرار می گیرد و خوانده نمی شود، همچون خواب، خواجه، خوارزم، خوار، خوراک، خوردن، خورش، خواسته، خواهش، خواهر، خواه، خوان، خواندن، آخوند، خود، خویش، نخود، خوش.

Contraction:

تخفیف: گاهی جهت آسانی تلفظ برخی حروف کلمات حذف می شود و این عمل را تخفیف و کلمه ای که حرف از آن افتاده را مخفف می گوییم: اگر:گر - از: ز - بازارگان:بازرگان - بهتر: به - بدتر: بتر - بیرون: برون چهاریک: چارک - خاموش: خموش - دیگر: دگر - راه: ره - روباه: روبه سیاه: سیه - قنددان: قندان - گوهر: گهر - من را: مرا - نیکو: نکو هم او: همو.

تخفیف را قاعده ی معین نیست و باید از اهل زبان یا کتب لغت آموخت.

Year

یک سال چهار فصل دارد. هر فصل سه ماه دارد.

بهار /bahâr/ اولین فصل سال است . ماه های فصل بهار:

Farvardin	فروردین
Ordibehesht	اردیبهشت
Khordâd	خرداد

تابستان /tâbestân/ فصل دوم سال است . ماه های فصل تابستان:

Tir	تیر
Mordâd	مرداد
Shahrivar	شهریور

پاییز /pâeiz/ فصل سوم سال است. ماه های فصل پاییز:

Mehr	مهر
Abân	آبان
Azar	آذر

زمستان /zemestân/ فصل چهارم است. ماه های فصل زمستان:

Dey	دی
Bahman	بهمن
Esfand	اسفند

Days of the week:

Saturday: /shanbeh/ شنبه

Sunday: /yekshanbeh/ یکشنبه

Monday: /doshanbeh/ دوشنبه

Tuesday: /seshanbeh/ سه شنبه

Wednesday: /chahârshanbeh/ چهارشنبه

Thursday: /panjshanbeh/ پنج شنبه

Friday: /jom'eh/ جمعه

Improve your writing: Write the sentences.

شنبه اولین روز کاری اَست.

....

من شما را سه شنبه بعد از ظهر میبینم.

....

دیانا برای خرید نان چهارشنبه به نانوایی میرود.

....

Colors

The world knows eight colors as Iranian or Persian color. The word for *color* is رنگ /*rang*/, and colors like other adjectives come after nouns.

English	Transliteration	Persian
white	sefid	سفید
black	Siya/meshki	سیاه/مشکی
Green	sabz	سبز
Blue	âbi	آبی
Red	ghermez	قرمز
Yellow	zard	زرد
Brown	Ghahve'i	قهوه ای
Grey	khâkestari	خاکستری
Beige	bezh	بژ
Cream	kerem	کرم
Orange	Nârenji	نارنجی
Pink	surati	صورتی
Violet	benafsh	بنفش
Gold	talâei	طلایی
Silver	noghre'i	نقره ای
Light	rowshan	روشن
A lighter shade	kam-rang	کم رنگ
Dark	tire	تیره
A darker shade	por-rang or sir	پررنگ یا سیر

www.persianbell.com

Numbers:

Unlike the Persian alphabet, Persian numbers are written from left to right. The word for *number* is عدد /adad/, with the broken plural اعداد /a'dād/.

Another word نمره /nomré/ (plural, نمرات *nómarāt*, occasionally نمره ها) and an original Persian word as شماره /shomāre/ 'number' are also used.

One	1	Yek	۱	یک
Two	2	Do	۲	دو
Three	3	Se	۳	سه
Four	4	chahâr	۴	چهار
Five	5	Panj	۵	پنج
Six	6	Shesh	۶	شش
Seven	7	Haft	۷	هفت
Eight	8	Hasht	۸	هشت
Nine	9	Noh	۹	نه
Ten	10	Dah	۱۰	ده
Eleven	11	Yâzdah	۱۱	یازده
Twelve	12	Davâzdah	۱۲	دوازده
Thirteeen	13	Sizdah	۱۳	سیزده
Fourteen	14	Chahârdah	۱۴	چهارده

English	Number	Transliteration		Persian
Fifteen	15	Pâanzdah	۱۵	پانزده
Sixteen	16	Shânzdah	۱۶	شانزده
Seventeen	17	Hefdah	۱۷	هفده
Eighteen	18	Hejdah	۱۸	هجده
Nineteen	19	Nuzdah	۱۹	نوزده
Twenty	20	Bist	۲۰	بیست
Thirty	30	Si	۳۰	سی
Fourty	40	Chehel	۴۰	چهل
Fifty	50	Panjâh	۵۰	پنجاه
Sixty	60	Shast	۶۰	شست
Seventy	70	Haftâd	۷۰	هفتاد
Eighty	80	Hashtâd	۸۰	هشتاد
Ninty	90	Navad	۹۰	نود
One Hundred	100	Yek sad	۱۰۰	صد
Two Hundred	200	Devist	۲۰۰	دویست
Three Hundred	300	Sisad	۳۰۰	سیصد
Four Hundred	400	Chahârsad	۴۰۰	چهارصد
Five Hundred	500	Pânsad	۵۰۰	پانصد
Six Hundred	600	Sheshsad	۶۰۰	ششصد
Seven Hundred	700	Haftsad	۷۰۰	هفتصد
Eight Hundred	800	Hashtsad	۸۰۰	هشتصد
Nine Hundred	900	Nohsad	۹۰۰	نهصد
One Thousand	1,000	yekHezâr	۱۰۰۰	هزار

Improve your writing: Write the sentences.

محمود ۳ برادر دارد.

....

روزهای هفته ۷ روز می باشد.

....

آرمیتا در روستا ۱۸ مرغابی دارد.

....

گردنبند قاصدک ۶۰ مهره تزیینی دارد.

....

دیروز فریبرز ۲۱۵ صفحه تایپ کرد.

....

عدد ۱۰۰۰ بزرگتر از عدد ۹۰۰ می باشد.

....

از عدد ۷۰ تا ۸۰ بشمارید.

....

عدد ۱۰۰ کوچکترین عدد سه رقمی است.

....

Learning Time

In **telling time**, normally the 12-hour set is used, not the 24-hour set. The 24-hour set is used in the Army and the media news broadcast. The cardinal numbers 1 to 12 are used for this purpose.

If you want to ask for the time in Persian, you only need to remember this formula:

/bebakhshid, sâ'at chand ast?/ ؟ببخشید، ساعت چند است
"Excuse me, what time is it?"

Remember that the word ساعت means 'watch, clock, time, hour.' The phrase in replying to asking the time is ساعت number است:

It is nine o'clock /sâ'at noh ast/. ساعت نه است.

Usually the word "ربع" /rob/ 'a quarter' and "نیم" /nim/ 'a half' are used; but the words "دقیقه" /daghighe/ 'minute' and ثانیّه /sâniyye/ 'second' are also used profusely:

/sâ'at do-vo nim ast/ .ساعت دو و نیم است
"It is two-thirty." (Literally, 'ten and a half')

As we can see, between the hour and the fraction the linking –o– ('and') intervenes. However, if the time said is before the hour, the link is dropped and the word "کم"/kam/ 'less, short, shy' follows the fraction:

/sâ'at yek rob' kam ast/ .ساعت یک، ربع کم است
It is quarter to one (Literally, "it is one, a quarter shy').

A.M. is صبح /sobh/ 'morning' and P.M. is بعد از ظهر /ba'd az zohr/ 'afternoon', both of which follow the number, linked by *ezâfe*:

ساعت پنج بعد از ظهر است. /sâ'at panj-e ba'd az zohr ast/

"It is five P.M."

In Persian the word for "midnight" doesn't exclusively refer to 12 A.M., but to all the hours between twelve A.M. and the sunrise. Therefore, if the time is between twelve and the sunrise (including twelve itself), it is referred to as نصف شب /nesf-e shab/ or (formally) نیمه شب /nime shab/ 'midnight':

ساعت دو و ربع نصف شب است. /sâ'at do-vo rob-e nesf-e shab ast/

"It is three-thirty A.M."

The word for 'noon' is "ظهر" /zohr/. Between ظهر and four or five P.M. (depending on the season and how soon or late the sun sets) is usually referred to as بعد از ظهر /ba'd az zohr/. Between those hours and the sunset, while the sky is still bright enough is usually referred to as عصر /asr/. The word for 'sunset' is غروب /ghorub/ or مغرب /maghreb/, which also means 'dusk.' A word for 'dawn' as بامداد /bâmdâd/ is used exclusively formally. The spoken word is almost always صبح /sobh/ 'morning'.

For an ambiguous time, span between the sunrise and noon is پیش از ظهر /pish az zohr/, or قبل از ظهر /ghabl az zohr/. Therefore, قبل از ظهر می بینمت /ghabl az zohr mi binamat/ means "I'll see you some time before noon," but it is normally closer to noon than to the sunrise. Normally the time between the sunrise and ten o'clock is referred to as صبح /sobh/ 'morning.'

After learning the basics about how to tell time in Persian, let's talk about the time adverbs. Here are some examples:

Right now, همین الان /hamin al'ân/

Currently در حال حاضر /dar hâle hazer/

Soon بزودی /bezoodi/

Almost تقریباً /taghriban/

Anytime هر زمان/هر وقت /har zaman/har vaght/

As soon as possible در اسرع وقت /dar asra'e vaqt/

Here are more examples:

"Come right now", (hamin al'ân biâ.") همین الان بیا.

من شما را بزودی خواهم دید.

I will see you soon. (man shomâ râ be zoodi khâham did).

Mathematical sign:

Mathematical sign: +, =, ÷, −, × نشانه های ریاضی:

Multiplication:	/zarb/	ضرب
Sum:	/be ezafe/	جمع
Minus:	/menha/	منها
Division:	/taqsim/	تقسیم
Equal:	/mosavi/	مساوی

Improve your writing: Write the sentences.

یک به اضافه دو مساوی است با سه   ۱+۲=۳

....

شش منهای سه مساوی است با سه   ۶-۳=۳

....

ده تقسیم بر دو مساوی است با دو   ۱۰÷۲=۵

....

چهار ضرب در سه مساوی است با دوازد   ۴×۳=۱۲

....

Reading and Writing

بخوانیم

و

بنویسیم

Practice Reading

and Writing

Text 1

نوروز

به روز اول سال جدید، نوروز می گوییم. نوروز عید مردم ایران است. مردم کشور ما قبل از نوروز خانه های خود را تمیز و پاکیزه می کنند.

انواع حبوبات و غلّات مانند گندم، جو، عدس و لوبیا را می کارند و تا روز ۱۳ آنها را نگه می دارند. مردم در روز اول نوروز سبزی پلو با ماهی می خورند.

در نوروز به دیدن یکدیگر می رویم و از بیماران دیدار می کنیم. از یک نوروز تا نوروز دیگر یکسال است.

Text 2

چهار فصل

هر سال چهار فصل دارد: بهار، تابستان، پاییز، زمستان.

در بهار هوا کم کم گرم می شود. درختان برگ و شکوفه می دهند. عیدنوروز، روز اول بهاراست. آیا می دانید ماه های فصل بهار چه نام دارد؟

بعد از بهار نوبت تابستان است. در این فصل، کشاورزان گندم و جو را درو می کنند. بچّه ها، شنا کردن در تابستان را دوست دارند.

پاییز فصل سوم سال است. برگ بعضی درختان زرد می شود و می ریزد. مهر، ماه اول پاییز، ماه شروع مدرسه است.

آخرین فصل سال، زمستان است. زمستان را با برف و سرما می شناسیم.

Text 3

معلّم

روزی که به مدرسه آمدیم خواندن و نوشتن نمی دانستیم. از همان روزهای اول معلّم مهربان ما را راهنمایی کرد. او به ما خواندن و نوشتن یاد داد.

او به ما یاد داد که با دوست خود مهربان باشیم، پاکیزه باشیم تا بیمار نشویم، به پدر و مادر خود احترام بگذاریم، دیگران را دوست داشته باشیم و به آنها کمک کنیم.

ما از معلّم خود سپاسگذاریم که به ما خواندن و نوشتن را یاد داد. از او سپاسگذاریم که مانند پدر و مادری مهربان به ما کارهای خوب و درس زندگی آموخت.

مثل خورشید

در یک شب مهتابی، من و پدرم به آسمان نگاه می کردیم. پدرم پرسید:

ثریّا جان آیا می دانی چه چیزی باعث روشن شدن زمین می شود؟

من چند ثانیه فکر کردم و گفتم: نور ماه.

پدر گفت: آفرین دخترم نور ماه در شب مثل نور خورشید در روز باعث روشن شدن زمین می شود.

من آن شب مهتابی را فراموش نمی کنم.

Text 5

میهن ما

کشور ما ایران است. ما در ایران زندگی می کنیم. کشور ما شهرها و روستاهای بسیاری دارد. دریا، کوهستان ها و دشت های فراوان دارد. بعضی از مردم کشور ما در روستاها و بعضی در شهرها زندگی می کنند.

کشور ایران با پیشینه و تاریخ غنی در کنار موقعیت جغرافیایی چهار فصل خود، آثار تاریخی و طبیعی حیرت‌انگیزی را در خود جای داده است؛ که میلیون‌ها گردشگر داخلی و خارجی از آنها دیدن می‌کنند.

تخت جمشید، نمادی از شکوه و عظمت در ایران باستان، یکی از مهم‌ترین اسناد تاریخ تمدن در جهان و یادگار پادشاهان هخامنشی از ۲۵۰۰ سال پیش در ایران است.

ما در هر جا که زندگی می کنیم میهن خود را دوست داریم.

Text 6

حلزون

آیا حَلَزون دیده ای؟ حَلَزون ها بدنی نرم دارند. بیشتر آنها، یک صدف دارند که به پشتشان چسبیده است. هر وقت حَلَزون احساس ترس می کند، همه بدنش را داخل این صدف می برد. حَلَزون خیلی آرام حرکت می کُند و هنگام حرکت، سر و بدنش از صدف بیرون اَست.

صبح ها اَگر کنار سبزه ها و مزرعه ها قدم بزنید، تعداد زیادی حلزون می بینید. حَلَزون وقتی حَرِکت می کُنَد، اثرش روی زمین یا هر جای دیگری باقی می مانَد. برای همین اَست که به آسانی، راه برگشت را پیدا می کُند.

آیا می دانستید به حلزون حیوان خانه به دوش می گویند؟

Text 7

سفر دلپذیر

زنگ آخر بود. خانم آموزگار پرسید:

کدام یک از شما تابستان گذشته به مسافرت رفته اید؟

مهشید دست بلند کرد و گفت: "اجازه! تابستان گذشته با پدر، مادر و برادرم به شهر رشت رفتیم. از دیدن جنگل ها، چشمه ها و شالیزارها لذّت بردیم. آن جا هوای خوب و دلپذیری داشت".

برادرم گفت: "کاش می توانستم هرچه را که می بینم بنویسم".

مادرم گفت: "وقتی به مدرسه بروی، نوشتن را یاد می گیری اما تا آن زمان هر چه را دیدی نقّاشی کن".

آزادی

پرندگان از این درخت به آن درخت می پرند آواز می خوانند برای خود و جوجه هایشان لانه درست می کنند و به آن ها غذا می دهند.

پرندگان از اینکه آزاد هستند لذّت می برند امّا بعضی مردم آن ها را در قفس زندانی می کنند. پرندگانی که در قفس زندانی هستند نمی توانند لانه بسازند و اَز درختی به درخت دیگر بپرند. همان طور که پرندگان برای آزادی خود تلاش می کنند انسان هم دوست دارد که آزاد زندگی کند.

آزادی انسان با آزادی پرندگان فرق دارد. ما آزاد نیستیم که هرکاری می خواهیم انجام دهیم. قانون تعیین می کند که آزادی ما چقدر اَست.

Text 9

عید قربان

هرسال مسلمانانی که توانایی دارند، از همه جای دنیا به زیارت خانه خدا می روند. خانه خدا یا کعبه در شهر مکه است. مسلمانان در مکّه، مراسم حج به جا می آورند. مراسم حج چند روز طول می کشد. در یکی ازاین روزها گوسفند، شتر یا گاوی را در راه خدا قربانی می کنند. که نام این روز را عید قُربان گذاشته اند. هرسال در این روزمسلمانان در مکّه جمع می شوند تا همبستگی خود را به تمام دنیا نشان دهند. عید قُربان از عیدهای بزرگ مسلمانان اَست.

Text 10

باغ پسته

اَبوذر پسردایی حنا و حامد اَست. پدر ابوذر باغبان اَست. او یک باغ بزرگ پسته در روستا دارد. باغ او مقدار زیادی پسته می دهد. پدر ابوذر به خوبی از درختان باغ مواظبت می کند. اَبوذر در آبیاری و سمپاشی درخت ها به پدرش کمک می کند. وقتی که پسته ها می رسد ابوذر وپدرش پسته ها را می چینند وبعد آن ها را برای فروش به شهر می برند.

New Words

كلمات جديد

Practice New Words

English	Translit	Persian	English	Translit	Persian
				آ	
Pollution	Âludegi	آلودگی	Sprinkler	Âbpâsh	آب پاش
Education	Âmuzesh	آموزش	Juicy	Âbdâr	آبدار
Song	Âvâz	آواز	Waterfall	Âbshâr	آبشار
Iron	Âhan	آهن	Juice	Âb mive	آب میوه
Future	Âyande	آینده	Climate	Âb o havâ	آب و هوا
Mirror	Âyne	آینه	Apartment	Âpârtemân	آپارتمان
Bedroom	Otâgh khâb	اتاق خواب	Brick	Âjor	آجر
Iron	Otu	اتو	Nuts	Âjil	آجیل
Rent, Lease	Ejâre	اجاره	Ethics	Âdâb	آداب
Permission	Ejâze	اجازه	Relief	Ârâmesh	آرامش
Respect	Ehterâm	احترام	Grave	Ârâmgâh	آرامگاه
Feeling	Ehsâs	احساس	Make-up	Ârâyesh	آرایش
Office	Edâre	اداره	Barbershop	Ârâyeshgâh	آرایشگاه
Value	Arzesh	ارزش	Barber	Ârâyeshgar	آرایشگر
Europe	Orupâ	اروپا	Liberty	Âzâdi	آزادی
Saw	Arre	ارّه	Easy	Âsân	آسان
To marry	Ezdevâj kardan	ازدواج کردن	Elevator	Âsânsor	آسانسور
Horse	Asb	اسب	Sky	Âsemân	آسمان
Toy	Asbâb bâzi	اسباب بازی	Broth	Âsh	آش
Spaghetti	Espâgeti	اسپاگتی	To drink	Âshâmidan	آشامیدن
Professor	Ostâd	استاد	Kitchen	Âshpazkhâneh	آشپزخانه
Pool	Estakhr	استخر	Sun	Âftâb	آفتاب
Relax	Esterâhat	استراحت			

English	Transliteration	Persian	English	Transliteration	Persian
Almond	Bâdâm	بادام	Use	Estefâde	استفاده
Market	Bâzâr	بازار	Note, Bill	Eskenâs	اسکناس
Club	Bâshgâh	باشگاه	Mistake	Eshtebâh	اشتباه
Garden	Bâgh	باغ	Problem	Eshkâl	اشکال
Zoo	Bâgh vahsh	باغ وحش	Things; Objects	Ashyâ'	اشیا
Up	Bâlâ	بالا	Members	A'zâ	اعضا
Body	Badan	بدن	Stay	Eghâmat	اقامت
Without	Bedun	بدون	Economy	Eghtesâd	اقتصاد
Badness	Ba'di	بعدی	Words	Alfâz	الفاظ
For	barâye	برای	But	Ammâ	اما
To take	Bardâshtan	برداشتن	This year	Emsâl	امسال
To take away to win	Bordan	بردن	Facilities	Emkânât	امکانات
Brush	Boros	برس	Properties	Amlâk	املاک
Cut, Slice	Boresh	برش	Safe	Amn	امن
Snowy	Barfi	برفی	Hope	Omid	امید
Electricity	Bargh	برق	Pomegranate	Anâr	انار
Leaf	Barg	برگ	To do	Anjâm dâdan	انجام دادن
Program, Schedule	Barnâme	برنامه	Drop	Andâkhtan	انداختن
Rice	Berenj	برنج	Size	Andâze	اندازه
Lamb	Barre	بره	Safety	Imeni	ایمنی
To cut	Boridan	بریدن	Here	Injâ	این جا
Large	Bozorg	بزرگ		ب	
To depend	Bastegi dâshtan	بستگی داشتن	Wind	Bâd	باد

English	Translit	Persian	English	Translit	Persian
Hospital	Bimârestân	بیمارستان	To close	Bastan	بستن
Illness	Bimâri	بیماری	Ice cream	Bastani	بستنی
International	Beynolmelali	بین المللی	Parcel, Closed, Package	Baste	بسته
	پ		Many, very	Besyâr	بسیار
Cloth	Pârche	پارچه	Then	Ba'd	بعد
Last year	Pârsâl	پارسال	Later	Ba'dan	بعدا
Park	Pârk kardan	پارک کردن	Some	Ba'zi	بازی
Parking	Pârking	پارکینگ	The rest, Remaining	Baghiyye	بقیه
Passport	Pâsport	پاسپورت	Ticket	Belit	بلیت
Envelope	Pâkat	پاکت	Building	Banâ	بنا
End	Pâyân	پایان	Port	Bandar	بندر
Capital	Pâytakht	پایتخت	Smell	Boo	بو
down, under	Pâyin	پایین	Kiss	Buse	بوسه
To cook	Pokhtan	پختن	Boulevard	Bulvâr	بولوار
To accept	Paziroftan	پذیرفتن	Best	Behtarin	بهترین
Full	Por	پُر	left behind	Be jâ mândan	به جا ماندن
Feather	Par	پَر	Hygienic	Behdâshti	بهداشتی
Payment	Pardâkht	پرداخت	Impolite	Bi adab	بی ادب
To ask	Porsidan	پرسیدن	To be awake	Bidâr budan	بیدار بودن
To fill	Por kardan	پر کردن	outside	Birun	بیرون
Bird	Parande	پرنده	More	Bishtar	بیشتر
Flight	Parvâz	پرواز	Earnest, Deposit	Beyâ'ne	بیعانه
Physician	Pezeshk	پزشک	Patient	Bimâr	بیمار

ت

English	Transliteration	Persian
History	Târikh	تاریخ
Historical	Târikhi	تاریخی
Dark	Târik	تاریک
Taxi	Tâksi	تاکسی
Fever	Tab	تب
Congratulation	Tabrik	تبریک
Experience	Tajrobe	تجربه
Education	Tahsilât	تحصیلات
Persepolis	Takht-e Jamshid	تخت جمشید
Board	Takhte	تخته
Discount	Takhfif	تخفیف
Egg	Tokhm	تخم
Egg	Tokhm-e morgh	تخم مرغ
Traffic	Trâfik	ترافیک
Arrangement, Order	Tartib	ترتیب
To be afraid of	Tarsidan	ترسیدن
Crack	tarak	ترک
Term	Term	ترم
Thirsty	Teshne	تشنه
Encouragement	Tashvigh	تشویق
Accident	Tasadof	تصادف
To decide	Tasmim gereftan	تصمیم گرفتن

English	Transliteration	Persian
Medicine	Pezeshki	پزشکی
Post	Post	پست
Breast	Pestân	پستان
Post man	Postchi	پستچی
Pistachio	Peste	پسته
Behind, Back	Posht	پشت
Bridge	Pol	پل
Number	Pelâk	پلاک
Panther	Palang	پلنگ
Cooker	Polopaz	پلوپز
Stair	Pelle	پله
Cotton	Panbe	پنبه
Cheese	Panir	پنیر
Powder	Pudr	پودر
Coverage	Pushesh	پوشش
To wear	Pushidan	پوشیدن
Money	Pul	پول
Rich	Puldâr	پولدار
On foot	Piyâde	پیاده
Onion	Piyâz	پیاز
Pizza	Pitzâ	پیتزا
Shirt, Blouse	Pirâhan	پیراهن
History	Pishine	پیشینه

English	Transliteration	Persian	English	Transliteration	Persian
To sweep	Jâru kardan	جارو کردن	Picture, Photo	Tasvir	تصویر
Interesting	Jâleb	جالب	Amount, Number	Te'dâd	تعداد
Living, Creature	Jândâr	جاندار	Definition	Ta'rif	تعریف
New	Jadid	جدید	Repair	Ta'mir	تعمیر
Except	Joz	جز	Difference	Tafâvot	تفاوت
Search	Josto joo	جستجو	Pleasure, Fun, Entertainment	Tafrih	تفریح
Celebration	Jashn	جشن	About, Almost	Taghriban	تقریبا
Geography	Joghrâfi	جغرافی	Piece	Tekke	تکه
Volume	Jeld	جلد	Stamp	Tambr	تمبر
Session, Meeting	Jalase	جلسه	Practice	Tamrin	تمرین
Front	Jelo	جلو	Alligator	Temsâh	تمساح
On the whole, Overall	Jam'an	جمعا	To clean	Tamiz kardan	تمیز کردن
Sentence	Jomle	جمله	Body	Tan	تن
Sex, Quality, Goods	Jens	جنس	Lazy	Tanbal	تنبل
Forest, Jungle	Jangal	جنگل	Jar, Flagon, Carafe	Tong	تنگ
Barley	Jow	جو	Razor, Razor blade	Tigh	تیغ
Answer	Javâb	جواب	ث		
Young	javân	جوان	Second (Time)	Sâniye	ثانیه
Youth	Javâni	جوانی	ج		
Chicken	Juje	جوجه	Place	jâ	جا
Stockings, Socks	Jurâb	جوراب	To replace	Jâ be jâ kardan	جا به جا کردن
World	jahân	جهان	Road	Jâdde	جاده
Scream	jigh	جیغ	Broom	jâru	جارو

Carrying	Haml	حمل		**چ**	
Forward, Attack	Hamle	حمله	Print	Châp	چاپ
Senses	Havâs	حواس	Fat	Châgh	چاق
Astonishment	Heyrat	حیرت	Tea	Chây	چای
Animal	Heyvân	حیوان	Left	Chap	چپ
	خ		Leather	Charm	چرم
Foreign	Khâreji	خارجی	Glue	Chasb	چسب
Special	Khâs	خاص	Spring	Cheshme	چشمه
Memories	Khâterât	خاطرات	How	Chegune	چگونه
Soil	Khâk	خاک	Suitcase	Chamedân	چمدان
Aunt	Khâle	خاله	Several	Chandin	چندین
Empty	Khâli	خالی	Wood	Choob	چوب
Cream	Khâme	خامه	Because	Choon	چون
God	Khodâ	خدا	Crossroads	Chahâr râh	چهارراه
Service	khedmat	خدمت	Face	Chehre	چهره
Ruin, Destroyed	kharâb	خراب	Something	Chizi	چیزی
Date	Khormâ	خرما	China	Chin	چین
Exit	Khoruji	خروج		**ح**	
Rooster	khorus	خروس	Now	HâLâ	حالا
Shopping	Kharid	خرید	Certainly	Hâtman	حتما
To buy	Kharidan	خریدن	Even	Hattâ	حتی
Tired	Khaste	خسته	To talk	Harf zadan	حرف زدن
Dry	Khoshk	خشک	Sensitive	Hassâs	حساس
Dried fruit	khoshkbâr	خشکبار	Right	Hagh	حق

English	Transliteration	Persian
Drug, Medicine	Dâru	دارو
Pharmacy	Dârukhâne	داروخانه
Pharmacist	Dâru sâz	داروساز
Story	Dâstân	داستان
Hot	Dâgh	داغ
Wise	Dânâ	دانا
To know	Dânestan	دانستن
Knowledge	Dânesh	دانش
Student	Dâneshju	دانشجو
College, Faculty	Dâneshkade	دانشکده
University	Dâneshgâh	دانشگاه
Scientist	Dâneshmand	دانشمند
Seed, Grain	Dâne	دانه
Circle	Dâyere	دایره
Income	Darâmad	درآمد
To take out	Dar âvardan	درآوردن
Long, Tall	Derâz	دراز
Degree	Daraje	درجه
Lesson	Dars	درس
Percent	Darsad	درصد
Treatment	Darmân	درمان
Clinic	Darmângâh	درمانگاه
Lier	Doruq gu	دروغ گو

English	Transliteration	Persian
Line	khat	خط
Dangerous	khatarnâk	خطرناک
Pilot	khalabân	خلبان
Laugh	Khande	خنده
Cool, Cold	Khonak	خنک
Dormitory	Khâbgâh	خوابگاه
To sleep	Khâbidan	خوابیدن
To want	Khâstan	خواستن
To study, To read, To sing	kHândan	خواندن
To ask, To demand	Khâhesh kardan	خواهش کردن
Good	Khub	خوب
To feed	Khorândan	خوراندن
To eat	Khordan	خوردن
Stew	Khoresht	خورشت
Happy	Khoshhâl	خوشحال
Coloury	Khoshrang	خوشرنگ
Delicious	Khoshmaze	خوشمزه
Blood	Khon	خون
Cucumber	Khiyâr	خیار
Wet	Khis	خیس
	د	
Court	Dâdgâh	دادگاه
To give	Dâdan	دادن

English	Transliteration	Persian
Visit	Didâr	دیدار
To visit	Didan kardan	دیدن کردن
Other	Digar	دیگر

ذ

English	Transliteration	Persian
Bit	Zarre	ذره
Taste, Verve	Zowgh	ذوق

ر

English	Transliteration	Persian
Boss, Chief	re'is	رئیس
Easy	râhat	راحت
Right, True	Râst	راست
Truth teller	Râst gu	راست گو
To drive	Rândan	راندن
Driving	Rânandegi	رانندگی
Way	Râh	راه
Corridor	Râhro	راهرو
Guidance	Râhnamâyi	راهنمایی
Common	Râyej	رایج
Free of charge	Râyegân	رایگان
To reject	Rad kardan	رد کردن
Rose	Roz	رز
Restaurant	Resturân	رستوران
Custom	Rasm	رسم
Formal	Rasmi	رسمی
To investigate / To consider	Residegi kardan	رسیدگی کردن

English	Transliteration	Persian
Valley	Darre	دره
Sea	Daryâ	دریا
Lake	Daryâche	دریاچه
Thief	Dozd	دزد
To touch	Dast zadan	دست زدن
Handkerchief, Napkin	Dastmal	دستمال
Difficult	Doshvâr	دشوار
To invite	da'vat kardan	دعوت کردن
Time	Daf'e	دفعه
Doctor	Doktor	دکتر
Stomach, Heart	Del	دل
Dolor	Dolâr	دلار
Temperature	Damâ	دما
Again	Dobâre	دوباره
Bicycle	Docharkhe	دوچرخه
Far	Dur	دور
Course, Period	Dowre	دوره
Friend	Dust	دوست
Friendship	Dusti	دوستی
Government	Dowlat	دولت
To run	Davidan	دویدن
Village	Deh	ده
Diploma	Diplom	دیپلم
Religion	Din	دین

English	Transliteration	Persian
ز		
Rubbish, Garbage	Zobâle	زباله
Language, Tongue	Zabân	زبان
Linguist	Zabân shenâs	زبان شناس
To hit	Zadan	زدن
Clever	Zerang	زرنگ
Saffron	Za'ferân	زعفران
Time	Zamân	زمان
Earth, Ground	Zamin	زمین
Woman	Zan	زن
Bee	Zanbur	زنبور
Alive	Zende	زنده
Bell	Zang	زنگ
Couple	Zowj	زوج
Soon, early	Zud	زود
Many	Ziyâd	زیاد
Shrine	Ziyâratgâh	زیارتگاه
Loss	Ziyân	زیان
Olive	Zeyton	زیتون
Because	Zirâ	زیرا
ژ		
Jacket	Zhâkat	ژاکت
Gesture, Pose	Zhest	ژست

English	Transliteration	Persian
To reach	Residan	رسیدن
Performance	Raftâr	رفتار
Sweeper	Roftegar	رفتگر
Traffic	Raft o âmad	رفت و آمد
To dance	Raghsidan	رقصیدن
Variously colored	Rangârang	رنگارنگ
propagation	Ravâj	رواج
Spirit, mind Easy	Ravân	روان
Psychologist	Ravân shenâs	روان شناس
Fox	Rubâh	روباه
Opposite	Ru be ru	رو به رو
River	Rood Roodkhâne	رود، رودخانه
Newspaper	Ruznâme	روزنامه
Village	Rustâ	روستا
Scarf	Rusari	روسری
Method	Ravesh	روش
Light	Ro(w)shanâi	روشنایی
Oil	Ro(w)ghan	روغن
Mathematics	Riyâzi	ریاضی
To pour	Rikhyan	ریختن
Tiny	Riz	ریز
Beard	Rish	ریش
Root	Rishe	ریشه

س

English	Transliteration	Persian
Service	Servis	سرویس
To order	Sefâresh dâdan	سفارش دادن
Travel	Safar	سفر
Tablecloth	Sofre	سفره
Roof	Saghf	سقف
Residence	Sokunat	سکونت
Coin	Sekke	سکه
Dog	Sag	سگ
Health	Salâmati	سلامت
Direction	Samt	سمت
Age	Sen	سن
Stone	Sang	سنگ
Soup	Sup	سوپ
To burn	Sukhtan	سوختن
Benefit Interest	Sood	سود
Needle	Suzan	سوزن
Souvenir	So(w)ghâti	سوغاتی
Political	Siyâsi	سیاسی
Potato	Sibzamini	سیب زمینی
Garlic	Sir	سیر
Cigarette	Sigâr	سیگار
Tray	Sini	سینی
Question	So'âl	سوال
Seaside	Sâhel	ساحل
Building	Sâkhtemân	ساختمان
Bag	Sâk	ساک
Silent	Sâket	ساکت
Hall, saloon	Sâlon	سالن
Centimeter	Sântimetr	سانتی متر
Vegetables	Sabzijât	سبزیجات
Overtaking, precedence	Sebghat	سبقت
Star	Setâre	ستاره
To praise	Sotudan	ستودن
Column	Sotun	ستون
Barrier, Dam	Sad	سد
Soldier	Sarbâz	سرباز
Careless	Sar be havâ	سر به هوا
To slide, Glide	Sor khordan	سر خوردن
Slide	Sorsore	سرسره
Cancer	Saratân	سرطان
Vinegar	Serke	سرکه
Adventures	Sargozasht	سرگذشت
Amused, Busy	Sargarm	سرگرم
Cold	Sarmâ	سرما
Cypress	Sarv	سرو

English	Translit	Persian	English	Translit	Persian
					ش
Radiator	Shufâzh	شوفاژ	Branch	Shâkhe	شاخه
Husband	Shohar	شوهر	Poet	Shâ'er	شاعر
City	Shahr	شهر	Shampoo	Shâmpoo	شامپو
Fame	Shohrat	شهرت	Bravery	Shojâ'at	شجاعت
Milk	Shir	شیر(نوشیدنی)	Person	Shakhs	شخص
Lion	Shir	شیر(حیوان)	Personal	Shakhsi	شخصی
Faucet	Shir	شیر(لوله)	East	Shargh	شرق
Sweet	Shirin	شیرین	Cooperation Company	sherkat	شرکت
Glass	Shishe	شیشه	Beginning	shoru'	شروع
Chemistry	Shimi	شیمی	To wash	Shostan	شستن
Method	Shive	شیوه	Washing	Shost-o-shu	شست و شو
		ص	Poem poetry	She'r	شعر
Morning	Sobh	صبح	Failure	Shekast	شکست
Breakfast	Sobhâne	صبحانه	To break	Shekastan	شکستن
morning	Sobhgâh	صبحگاه	Fragile	Shkastani	شکستنی
To wait	Sabr kardan	صبر کردن	Chocolate	Shokolât	شکلات
Talk	Sohbat	صحبت	Crowded	Sholuqh	شلوغ
To call	Sedâ zadan	صدا زدن	North	Shomâl	شمال
Shell	Sadaf	صدف	To count	Shemordan	شمردن
Zero	Sefr	صفر	Candle	Sham'	شمع
Friendly	Samimi	صمیمی	Joking	Shukhi	شوخی
Chair	Sandali	صندلی	Salty	Shur	شور(غذا)
Box Cash	Sandugh	صندوق			

ع

English	Transliteration	Persian
Ordinary	'âddi	عادی
Emotional	'âtefi	عاطفی
Excellent	'âli	عالی
Strange	'ajib	عجیب
To appologize	Ozr khâstan	عذر خواستن
Width	'arz	عرض
Bride	'arus	عروس
Wedding	'arusi	عروسی
Mourning	'azâdâri	عزاداری
Member	'ozv	عضو
Picture, Photo	'aks	عکس
Interest	'alâghe	علاقه
Sign	'alâmat	علامت
In addition to	'alâve bar	علاوه بر
Reason	'ellat	علت
Science	'elm	علم
Age, Life	'omar	عمر
Vertical	'amoudi	عمودی
Public, General	'omumi	عمومی
Deep	'amigh	عمیق
Title, Topic	'onvân	عنوان
Visit an ill person	'ayâdat	عیادت

English	Transliteration	Persian
Industry	San'at	صنعت
Spruce	Seno(w)bar	صنوبر
Bill	Surat hesâb	صورت حساب

ض

English	Transliteration	Persian
Multiplication	Zarb	ضرب
Pulse	Zarabân	ضربان
Impact	Zarbe	ضربه
Weak	Za'if	ضعیف

ط

English	Transliteration	Persian
Floor	Tabaghe	طبقه
Nature	Tabi'at	طبیعت
Natural	Tabi'i	طبیعی
Side	Taraf	طرف
Taste	Ta'm	طعم
Gold	Tala	طلا
Length	Tul	طول
To go	Tey kardan	طی کردن

ظ

English	Transliteration	Persian
Dish, Container	Zarf	ظرافت
Delicate	Zarif	ظریف
Oppression	Zolm	ظلم
Suspicion	Zan	ظن
Emergence	Zohur	ظهور

English	Translit	Persian	English	Translit	Persian
					غ
France	Farânse	فرانسه	Cave	Ghâr	غار
Abundant	Farâvân	فراوان	Unaware	Ghâfel	غافل
Child	Farzand	فرزند	Gland	Ghodde	غده
Difference	Fargh	فرق	West	Gharb	غرب
From	Form	فرم	Booth	Ghorfe	غرفه
Order, Wheel	Farmân	فرمان	To sink	Ghargh kardan	غرق کردن
Ruler	Farmânravâ	فرمانروا	Pride	Ghorur	غرور
To sell	Forukhtan	فروختن	Strange	gharib	غریب
To land	Forud âmadan	فرود امدن	Sonnet	ghazal	غزل
Airport	forudgâh	فرودگاه	Sad	Ghamgin	غمگین
Seller	Forushande	فروشنده	Bud	Ghonche	غنچه
Culture	Farhang	فرهنگ	Rich, Full	Ghani	غنی
Poor	Faghir	فقیر	Absence	Gheybat	غیبت
To think	Fekr kardan	فکر کردن	Unauthorized	Gheyr-e mojâz	غیرمجاز
Metal	Felez	فلز			ف
Philosophy	Falsafe	فلسفه	Persian	Fârsi	فارسی
Hazelnut	Fandogh	فندق	Distance	Fâsele	فاصله
Footballer	Futbâlist	فوتبالیست	Factor, Bill	Fâctor	فاکتور
List	Fehrest	فهرست	To tell fortunes	Fâl gereftan	فال گرفتن
Menu	Fehrest ghazâ	فهرست غذا	Relatives	Fâmil	فامیل
To understand	Fahmidan	فهمیدن	Curl	Fer	فر
Physics	Fizik	فیزیک	Forgotten	Farâmush	فراموش
Film	Film	فیلم			

English	Translit	Persian	English	Translit	Persian
Sugar cup	Ghandân	قندان		**ق**	
Tribe	Ghowm	قوم	Frame	Ghâb	قبض
Coffee	Ghahve	قهوه	Pan, Casserole	Ghâblame	قابلمه
Coffee-House	Ghahve khâne	قهوه خانه	Murderer	Ghâtel	قاتل
Face	Ghiyâfe	قیافه	Continent	Ghârre	قاره
Scissors	Gheychi	قیچی	Frame	Ghâleb	قالب
Price	Gheymat	قیمت	Carpet	Ghâli	قالی
	ک		Law	Ghânun	قانون
Pine	Kâj	کاج	Boating	Ghâyegh savâri	قایق سواری
Palace	Kâkh	کاخ	Ago, before	Ghabl	قبل
Museum-palace	Kâkh muze	کاخ موزه	Height	Ghad	قد
Gift	Kâdo	کادو	Old, Ancient	Ghadimi	قدیمی
Postal card	Kârt postâl	کارت پستال	Koran	Ghor'ân	قرآن
Factory	Kâr khâne	کارخانه	To lend	Gharz dâdan	قرض دادن
To work	Kâr kardan	کار کردن	Century	Gharn	قرن
Workshop	Kârgâh	کارگاه	Beautiful	Ghashang	قشنگ
Worker	Kârgar	کارگر	Butcher	Ghassâb	قصاب
Director	Kârgardân	کارگردان	Train	Ghatâr	قطار
Report card	Kârnâme	کارنامه	Cage	Ghafas	قفس
I wish	Kâsh	کاش	Lock	Ghofl	قفل
To plant	Kâshtan	کاشتن	Heart	Ghalb	قلب
Paper	Kâghaz	کاغذ	Pen	Ghalam	قلم
Efficient, enough	Kâfi	کافی	Peak, Climax	Gholle	قله
Bologna	Kâlbâs	کالباس	Hard sugar	Ghand	قند

English	Transliteration	Persian	English	Transliteration	Persian
Control	Kontorol	کنترل	Truck	Kâmiyon	کامیون
Short	Kutâh	کوتاه	lettuce	Kâhu	کاهو
Kid	Kudak	کودک	Kabab	Kabâb	کباب
Jug, Pitcher	Kuze	کوزه	Match	Kebrit	کبریت
Cooler	Kuler	کولر	Coat	Kot	کت
That	Ke	که	Which	Kodâm	کدام
Quality	Keyfiyyat	کیفیت	Postal code	Kode posti	کد پستی
Kilo	Kiloo	کیلو	Tie	Kerâvât	کراوات
Kilometer	Kilumetr	کیلومتر	Sphere	Kore	کره
		گ	Butter	Kare	کره
Gas	Gâz	گاز	Farmer	Keshvarz	کشاورز
Cow	Gâv	گاو	To kill	Koshtan	کشتن
To put	Gozâshtan	گذاشتن	Raisin	Keshmesh	کشمش
Past	Gozashte	گذشته	Shoes	Kafsh	کفش
Cat	Gorbe	گربه	Crow	Kalâgh	کلاغ
Round	Gerd	گرد	Hat	Kolâh	کلاه
Tourism	Gardeshgari	گردشگری	Maid	Kolfat	کلفت
Necklace	Garanband	گردنبند	Cabbage	Kalam	کلم
Wall nut	Gerdu	گردو	Key	Kelid	کلید
Hungry	Gorosne	گرسنه	Little	Kam	کم
Gram	Geram	گِرم	Waist, Back	Kamar	کمر
Warm	Garm	گرم	Help	Komak	کمک
Group	Goruh	گروه	Unique	Kam nazir	کم نظیر

ل

English	Transliteration	Persian
lobby	Lâbi	لابی
Thin, Slender	Lâghar	لاغر
Turtle	Lâkposht	لاک پشت
Lamp	Lâmp	لامپ
Nest	Lâne	لانه
Layer	Lâye	لایه
Dairy products	Labaniyyât	لبنیات
Quilt	Lehâf	لحاف
Moment	Lahze	لحظه
To enjoy	Lazzat bordan	لذت بردن
To be kind to	Lotf kardan	لطف کردن
Word	Lafz	لفظ
Tools	Lavâzem	لوازم
Accent	Lahje	لهجه
Bachelor (degree)	Lisâns	لیسانس

م

English	Transliteration	Persian
Astonished, Opaque	Mât	مات
Market	Mâzhik	مازیک
Yogurt	Mâst	ماست
Car	Mâshin	ماشین
To rub	Mâlidan	مالیدن
Like, such as	Mânand	مانند

English	Transliteration	Persian
Report	Gozâresh	گزارش
expansion	Gostaresh	گسترش
Hungry	Goshne	گرسنه
Speech	Goftâr	گفتار
Dialogue	Goft-o gu	گفت و گو
Flower	Gol	گل
Mud	Gel	گل
Cauli flower	Gole kalam	گل کلم
Throat	Galu	گلو
Customs	Gomrok	گمرک
Capacity	Gonjâyesh	گنجایش
Wheat	Gandom	گندم
Tomato	Go(w)je farangi	گوجه فرنگی
Sheep	Gusfand	گوسفند
Ear	Gush	گوش
To listen	Gush kardan	گوش کردن
Smartphone, Headset	Gushi	گوشی
Cheek	Gune	گونه
Breed, Type	Gune	گونه
Speaker	Guyande	گوینده
Gem, Jewel, Nature	Gowhar	گوهر
Receiver	Girande	گیرنده
Cherry	Gilâs	گیلاس

English	Transliteration	Persian	English	Transliteration	Persian
Ground	Mohavvate	محوطه	Month, Moon	Mâh	ماه
Area	Mohit	محیط	Skillful	Mâher	ماهر
Various, Different	Mokhtalef	مختلف	Monthly	Mâhiyâne	ماهیانه
Special	Makhsus	مخصوص	Fishing	Mâhigiri	ماهیگیری
Duration	Moddat	مدت	Liquid	Mâye	مایع
Dean, Principle Manager	Modir	مدیر	Swimming trunk	Mâyo	مایو
Reference Refering	Morâje'e	مراجعه	Official	Ma'mur	مامور
Man	Mard	مرد	Happy	Mobârak	مبارک
Masculine	Mardâne	مردانه	To get an illness	Mobtalâ shodan	مبتلا شدن
People	Mardom	مردم	Price	Mablagh	مبلغ
Of good quality	Marqhub	مرغوب	Meter	Metr	متر
Center	Markaz	مرکز	Underground Subway	Metro	مترو
Marble	Marmar	مرمر	Clerk, Person in charge	Motesaddi	متصدی
Pearl	Morvârid	مروارید	Numerous	Mote'added	متعدد
To review	Morur kardan	مرور کردن	Text	Matn	متن
Annoyance	Mozâhem	مزاحم	Diverse	Motenavve'	متنوع
Salary, Wage	Mozd	مزد	For example,	Masalan	مثلا
Question Issue	Mas'ale	مسئله	Triangle	Mosallas	مثلث
In charge Responsible	Mas'ul	مسئول	Allowed Authorized	Mojâz	مجاز
Game	Mosâbeghe	مسابقه	To be forced	Majbur budan	مجبور بودن
Passenger	Mosâfer	مسافر	Status	Mojassame	مجسمه
Travel	Mosâferat	مسافرت	Set, Collection	Majmu'e	مجموعه
Straight	Mostaghim	مستقیم	Regional	Mahalli	محلی

English	Transliteration	Persian	English	Transliteration	Persian
Meaning	Ma'nâ	معنا	Mosque	Masjed	مسجد
Shop	Maghâze	مغازه	Ridiculous	Maskhare	مسخره
Opposite	Moghâbel	متقابل	Muslim	Mosalmân	مسلمان
Comparison	Moghâyese	مقایسه	Path	Masir	مسیر
Amount	Meghdâr	مقدار	Consultant	Moshâver	مشاور
Holy	Moghaddas	مقدس	Observe	Moshâhede	مشاهده
Destination	Maghsad	مقصد	Specifications	Moshakhkhasât	مشخصات
To meet	Molâghât kardan	ملاقات کردن	Problem	Moshkel	مشکل
National	Melli	ملی	Famous	Mashhur	مشهور
Forbidden	Mamnu'	ممنوع	Consumption	Masraf	مصرف
Grateful	Mamnun	ممنون	Study	Motâle'e	مطالعه
Proper	Monâseb	مناسب	Issue, Topic	Matlab	مطلب
Awaiting	Montazer	منتظر	Sure	Motma'en	مطمئن
In order	Monazzam	منظّم	Contemporary	Mo'âser	معاصر
Motor	Motor	موتور	Exempted	Mo'âf	معاف
Museum	Muze	موزه	Treatment	Mo'âleje	معالجه
Temporary	Movaghghat	موقّت	To examine	Mo'âyene	معاینه
Time Occasion	Mo(w)ghe'	موقع	Mild Temperate	Mo'tadel	معتدل
Immigrant	Mohâjer	مهاجر	To appologize	Ma'zerat khâstan	معذرت خواستن
Moon light	Mahtâb	مهتاب	Famous	Ma'ruf	معروف
Kindness	Mehrabâni	مهربانی	Knowledge	Ma'lumât	معلومات
Important	Mohem	مهم	Architecture	Me'mâri	معماری
Guest	Mehmân	مهمان	Usually,	Ma'mulan	معمولا

English	Translit	Persian	English	Translit	Persian
Green pea	Nokhod farangi	نخود فرنگی	Party	Mehmâni	مهمانی
Ladder	Nardebân	نردبان	Engineer	Mohandes	مهندس
Soft	Narm	نرم	Nail	Mikh	میخ
Near	Nazdik	نزدیک	To desire	Meyl dâshtan	میل داشتن
Species	Nezhâd	نژاد	Million	Milyun	میلیون
Relation	Nesbat	نسبت	Miniature	Miniyâtor	مینیاتور
Prescription	Noskhe	نسخه	Fruit	Mive	میوه
Address	Neshâni	نشانی		ن	
Military	Nezâmi	نظامی	Genius	Nâbeghe	نابغه
Oil	Naft	نفت	Blind	Nâbinâ	نابینا
Curse	Nefrin	نفرین	Fingernail	Nâkhon	ناخن
Influence Penetration	Nofuz	نفوذ	Coconut	Nârgil	نارگیل
Precious Valuable	Nafis	نفیس	Sour orange	Nârenj	نارنگی
Mask	Neghâb	نقاب	Tangerine	Nârengi	نارنجی
Painter Artist	Naghghâsh	نقاش	Suddenly	Nâgahân	ناگهان
Painting	Naghghâshi	نقاشی	Name	Nâm	نام
Silver	Noghre	نقره	Fiance'	Nâmzad	نامزد
Role, Picture, Design	Naghsh	نقش	Engagement	Nâmzadi	نامزدی
To have a role in	Naghsh dâshtan	نقش داشتن	Letter	Nâme	نامه
Map	Naghshe	نقشه	Baker	Nânvâ	نانوا
An Iranian candy	Noghl	نقل	Result	Natije	نتیجه
Point	Nokte	نکته	Thread	Nakh	نخ
Worried	Negarân	نگران	Chick-pea	Nokhodchi	نخود چی

و

English	Transliteration	Persian
And	Va	وَ
To enter	Vâred shodan	وارد شدن
Really	Vâghe'an	واقعا
Vax	Vâks	واکس
To exist	Vojud dâshtan	وجود داشتن
Savage Wild	Vahshi	وحشی
Sport center Stadium	Varzeshgâh	ورزشگاه
Paper Sheet	Varaqhe	ورقه
Inflation	Varam	ورم
Entrance	Vorudi	ورودی
No entry	Vorud mamnu'	ورود ممنوع
weight	Vazn	وزن
To weigh	Vazn kardan	وزن کردن
To blow	Vazidan	وزیدن
Equipment	Vasâyel	وسایل
Middle	Vasat	وسط
Vehicle	Vasiley-e naghliye	وسیله نقلیه
Country	Vatan	وطن
Faithfull, Loyal	Vafâdar	وفادار
To have time	Vaght dâshtan	وقت داشتن
When	Vaghti	وقتی
Characteristic	Vizhegi	ویژگی
Maintenance	Negahdâri	نگهداری
Prayers	Namâz	نماز
To say, Prayers	Namâz khândan	نماز خواندن
Show	Namâyesh	نمایش
Exhibition	namâyeshgâh	نمایشگاه
Representative Agent	Namâyande	نماینده
Saltshaker	Namak pâsh	نمک پاش
Salt container	Namakdân	نمک دان
Instance	Nemune	نمونه
Mother	nane	ننه
New	Now	نو
Tape	Navâr	نوار
Light	Noor	نور
Nowruz	Nowruz	نوروز
Manuscript	Neveshte	نوشته
To drink	Nushidan	نوشیدن
Drink, Beverage	Nushidani	نوشیدنی
Type, Kind	No'	نوع
Author	Nevisande	نویسنده
Final	Nahâ'i	نهایی
Needy	Niyâzmand	نیازمند
Also	Niz	نیز
Goodness	Niki	نیکی

English	Translit	Persian
Meteorologist	Havâshenâs	هواشناسی
Wisdom	Hush	هوش
Carrot	Havij	هویج
Nothing	Hich	هیچ

ی

English	Translit	Persian
Memory	Yâd	یاد
To instruct, To teach	Yâd dâdan	یاد دادن
Note	Yâddâsht	یادداشت
To learn	Yâd gereftan	یاد گرفتن
Pal, Friend	Yâr	یار
Ruby	Yâghut	یاقوت
Ice	Yakh	یخ
Refrigerator	Yakhchâl	یخچال
Icy	Yakhi	یخی
Once	Yekbâr	یکبار
The same	Yeksân	یکسان
Slow	Yavâsh	یواش

ه

English	Translit	Persian
Hot dog	Hât dâg	هات داگ
Hotel	Hotel	هتل
Gift	Hadiye	هدیه
Never	Hargez	هرگز
Any time	Har vaght	هر وقت
Cost, Expense	Hazine	هزینه
Aware	Hoshyâr	هشیار
To push	Hol dâdan	هول دادن
Playmate	Hambâzi	همبازی
Hamburger	Hamberger	همبرگر
Also	Hamchenin	همچنین
Neighbour	Hamsâye	همسایه
Colleague	Hamkâr	همکار
Classmate	Hamkelâsi	همکلاسی
Always	Hamvâre	همواره
India	Hend	هند
Geometrical	Hendesi	هندسی
Watermelon	Hendevâne	هندوانه
Art	Honar	هنر
Artist	Honarmand	هنرمند
Yet, Still	Hanuz	هنوز
Airplane	Havâpeymâ	هواپیما

الفبای فارسی

برای

نوآموزان

حمید اسلامیان

www.ingramcontent.com/pod-product-compliance
Lightning Source LLC
Chambersburg PA
CBHW071854070526
44583CB00016B/1685